THE FOURTH PILLAR OF SUSTAINABILITY

Culture's essential role in public planning

BY JON HAWKES

FOR THE CULTURAL
DEVELOPMENT NETWORK
VICTORIA

This book is published at the Humanities.com
a series imprint of the UniversityPress.com

First published in Australian in 2001 by
Common Ground Publishing Pty Ltd in association
with the Cultural Development Network (Vic).
www.theHumanities.com

Reprinted 2003, 2004
Copyright © Jon Hawkes and the
Cultural Development Network (Vic) 2001

All rights reserved. Apart from fair dealing for the purposes
of study, research, criticism or review as permitted under the
Copyright Act, no part of this book may be reproduced by
any process without written permission from the publisher.

National Library of Australia Cataloguing-in-Publication data:

Hawkes, Jon, 1946- .
The fourth pillar of sustainability:
culture's essential role in public planning.

Bibliography.
ISBN 1 86335 049 7.

ISBN 1 86335 050 0 (PDF).

1. Social policy. 2. Arts and society. 3. Cultural policy.
I. Cultural Development Network of Victoria. II. Title.

361.25

Cover and text designed by Dianna Wells Design
Printed in Australia by Mercury Printeam

The Cultural Development Network is supported by:

Contact Details: Judy Spokes, Executive Officer
Cultural Development Network (Vic)
judspo@melbourne.vic.gov.au

FOREWORD

Culture is one of those omnibus terms like democracy or environment which embraces many different usages employed by many different people for many different purposes. It thus defies precise definition. It can be seen to represent very many of the intangible aspects of our values, customs and patterns of life that are often ignored in government thinking and action. If the understanding or definition is a broad one, it represents profoundly important aspects of any society. There is therefore a critical need to reintroduce the notion of culture into the language of politicians and bureaucrats.

This is what Jon Hawkes has set out to do in this paper. The paper explores the many different ways that culture affects and relates to patterns of human activities and policy realms. It concludes with a discussion of the practical ways in which notions of culture can be applied to public policy and examples of models that can be drawn upon from around the world.

The notion of cultural policy is a largely a foreign one in Anglo-Celtic countries. There are certainly arts policies and no one would belittle their importance. Arts policies should have an honoured place in any cultural policy. But a cultural policy, or a cultural framework as Jon Hawkes prefers to argue, should seek to do more. Its aim should be to enrich the lives of all citizens in many different ways and to protect and enhance the rights of citizens to freedom of expression and access to information and resources.

It should therefore begin with a set of principles or objectives which are widely available for discussion. Jon Hawkes lists the objectives for cultural policy in Sweden as an example. These and other alternatives discussed provide an excellent foundation for the development of objectives or principles relevant to Australia.

Once a set of principles has been agreed, the next step is to determine the policy areas to which a particular cultural policy will apply. This is important because there are many options, some which spill over into social or environmental policy. The choice of policy areas should be pragmatic but also needs to be fully justified. Jon opts for a framework or sieve applicable to all areas of public policy rather than for the development of a specific cultural policy. I would argue for both. Whatever the merits of either argument, there is scope and material enough in this paper to stimulate a good debate within any government body about the best way to proceed.

The last step is to apply the agreed principles to the chosen policy areas to determine what new policies or reinforcement or modification of existing policies might be proposed.

In these different ways, the ideas which Jon Hawkes is canvassing and the debate which he is opening up can be turned to practical advantage. I commend the paper to you and hope that it will lead to much new thinking and policy innovation.

DAVID YENCKEN

CONTENTS

Preface	vi
Summary	vi
Introduction	1
CHAPTER 1 The meaning of culture	3
Establishing a useful description	3
Culture in everyday useage	4
Values	4
Culture and government	7
Developments in the public planning arena	9
CHAPTER 2 The application of culture	11
Sustainable development	11
Wellbeing	12
Diversity	13
Globalisation and distinctiveness	15
Engagement, active citizenship and civil society	16
Creativity and innovation	17
Community building, cohesion, capacity and social capital	18
Liveability and quality of life	19
Identity and character	19
Belonging and a sense of place	20
Ethics and morality	21
Progress and development	21
Vitality	22
The arts	23
Ecologically sustainable development and the triple bottom line	25
CHAPTER 3 The results of culture	27
Restructuring	27
Education and training	28
Communications and public affairs	29
The constructed environment and public facilities	30
Arts	30
History and heritage	30
Recreation and leisure	31
Sport	31

A 'Cultural Framework'	32
Cultural indicators	33
Content	33
Practice	33
Results	33
Specific policy development	34
Instrumental initiatives	37
Cultural action	37
Conclusion	**38**
Appendix 1: Public planning frameworks	**39**
Citizenship and deliberative democracy	39
Community capacity building	40
Community indicators	40
Ecologically Sustainable Development and Local Agenda 21	40
Genuine Progress Indicator	42
Good practice	43
Integrated local area planning (ILAP)	43
Quality of life, wellbeing, life satisfaction & liveability	43
Subjective indicators	44
Objective indicators	44
Social auditing	46
Social capital	46
Sustainable development	47
Sustainable development indicators (SDIs)	47
Triple bottom line	47
Whole of government	47
Appendix 2: The Action Plan from 'The Power of Culture'	**48**
Preamble	48
Recognizes the following principles	49
The Conference in consequence affirms that	49
Policy objectives recommended to member states	51
1: To make cultural policy one of the key components of development strategy.	51
2: Promote creativity and participation in cultural life.	52

  3: *Reinforce policy and practice to safeguard and enhance the cultural heritage, tangible and intangible, moveable and immoveable, and to promote cultural industries.* 52

  4: *Promote cultural and linguistic diversity in and for the information society.* 54

  5: *Make more human and finacial resources available for cultural development.*

 Recommendations to the Director-General of UNESCO 55

Appendix 3: Arts indicators **57**

 The arts community's connections to larger community issues and expectations 57

 Community perceptions of the arts 57

 Community expectations of the arts community 57

 Connections across groups/boundaries 58

 Diversity of opportunities for arts participation, including opportunities for continuous and deepening participation 58

 Diversity of opportunities for youth and level and continuity of participation by youth 58

 The arts community's response to cultural diversity 58

 Vitality of arts offerings 59

 Health of the arts community 59

 Opportunities for vocational arts training 59

 Diversity of institutions involved in the arts, including non-traditional examples 59

 Arts community's engagement with celebration of heritage 60

 Sustainability of the arts community 60

 Municipal contribution 60

Appendix 4: About the author and the Network **61**

 The author 61

 The Cultural Development Network (Vic) 61

Bibliography **62**

PREFACE

This paper has been prepared for the Cultural Development Network (Vic). The brief under which it was commissioned called for the examination of the potential value of a specifically cultural perspective to the planning, service delivery and evaluation activities of local government. The title of this monograph is inspired by Yencken and Wilkinson who, in their book, *Resetting the Compass* (2000), support those asserting that there should be four pillars of sustainability.

SUMMARY

A society's values are the basis upon which all else is built. These values and the ways they are expressed are a society's culture. The way a society governs itself cannot be fully democratic without there being clear avenues for the expression of community values, and unless these expressions directly affect the directions society takes. These processes are culture at work.

Cultural vitality is as essential to a healthy and sustainable society as social equity, environmental responsibility and economic viability. In order for public planning to be more effective, its methodology should include an integrated framework of cultural evaluation along similar lines to those being developed for social, environmental and economic impact assessment.

INTRODUCTION

There is a growing recognition among those who influence the way our society manages itself that economic benchmarks alone are an insufficient framework upon which to evaluate progress or to plan for the future. This awareness has led to the development (and rediscovery) of a wide range of alternative ways of viewing and analysing the performance of a society[1]. All these new frameworks are based on a commitment to expanding the consciousness of what makes for a society that reflects and fulfils the aspirations of its citizens.

This paper will demonstrate that the concept of culture is an invaluable tool that has been largely ignored in these attempts to reconfigure the ways that governments plan the future and evaluate the past.

When culture is taken to denote the social production and transmission of values and meaning[2] and it is recognised that the expression of social purpose and aspiration is at the heart of the public planning process[3], then the connection between culture and planning becomes clearer. So also does the potential for the use of culture as a core element in the mechanisms that facilitate effective public planning.

The introduction of the concept of culture into the theoretical and operational frameworks of public affairs has an extraordinary range of potential benefits; for example:

— it formally identifies the aspirations and values of communities as being at the foundation of society;

— it puts a name to the profound undercurrent that has been recognised as influential in many (possibly most) of the developing paradigms: virtually all the revisionist planning templates are surrounded with the rhetoric of consultation, interaction, community initiative – this recognition that democracy requires that the active voices of communities be heard and accorded influence is a cultural phenomenon and can most readily be understood and dealt with from a cultural perspective;

— it brings clarity to the rather fuzzy concepts that have consistently impeded the practical application of planning theories: 'culture' gives a name to the processes we use to discuss our futures, evaluate our pasts, and act in the present;

— it brings together a range of concepts and issues that have, thus far, developed in parallel: wellbeing, cohesion, capacity, engagement, belonging, distinctiveness are all ideas that are being used in the current planning debates without any significant success in developing an intellectual or operationally functional model that integrates them. The concept of culture provides the intellectual tools with which a more effective structure can be built;

---

[1] See below, **'Developments in the public planning arena'** for a list of the main frameworks and Appendix 1 for brief descriptions of some of them.

[2] For a more comprehensive definition of culture see below, **'Establishing a useful description'**.

[3] For example, 'Values are the basis for action' from Gleeson, B. & Low, N *Australian Urban Planning: new challenges, new agendas* (2000) St Leonards, Allen & Unwin; page 217.

- it provides an improved theoretical model: one that has the capacity to integrate the full range of social relations and organisations within a framework that is comprehensive, accessible, flexible and standardisable;
- it makes it easier to clarify strategic objectives and implement strategic operations: because the concept of culture encompasses the means through which communities express their values, it makes it easier to conceive of ways of integrating public expression into planning processes;
- it improves the integration of public program management[4]: because the concept of culture encompasses all stages of the process, from the articulation of ideas through to their practical manifestation in the real world, it creates a context in which cultural priorities can be addressed, in a focussed way, throughout the public cycle – policy development, planning, implementation, evaluation.

In demonstrating how the concept of culture can be most effectively applied within the context of public planning, this paper will argue that:

- governments' useage and understanding of culture in their planning, service delivery and evaluation activities have been limited and counter-productive;
- carefully planned cultural action is essential for the achievement of sustainabilty and wellbeing;
- the engines of cultural production would operate most effectively through a singular and co-ordinated setting within government management structures;
- the development of a cultural framework through which all public planning can be evaluated is an essential step;
- active community participation in arts practice is an essential component of a healthy and sustainable society.

The paper is structured to reflect the three aspects of culture described in the first section below:

- **The meaning of culture**: a useful and useable description of culture is proposed; everyday useage of the term is examined; the growing awareness of the importance of social values being expressed and applied is noted; the ways that governments have dealt with culture is explored.
- **The application of culture**: the developing range of paradigms for examining society and assessing its performance are examined. The role that culture plays in each is identified.
- **The results of culture**: ways that a cultural perspective may be practically applied to the planning process are suggested and examined.

The main conclusion of this paper is that the new governance paradigms and views of what constitutes a healthy and sustainable society would be more effective if cultural vitality were to be included as one of the basic requirements, main conceptual tenets and overriding evaluation streams.

---

[4] See below, '**Restructuring**'.

Chapter 1

THE MEANING OF CULTURE

I start by proposing a description of culture that is useful in the public planning context; the duality of the everyday use of the term is highlighted; the growing awareness that social values have a critical function in governance is made clear; the continuing application of culture's dual useage in government thinking is tracked; and the way that, without refering to culture, concepts of meaning and purpose are being used in the emerging planning frameworks is demonstrated.

ESTABLISHING A USEFUL DESCRIPTION

The word culture is one of the most complex and contested words in the English language. So much so, that revisiting its meaning usually causes more heat than illumination. But revisit we must, if only to make it clear how I will apply the concept in this paper.

Without delving too deeply into the mass of scholarly literature that has developed around this word, two inter-related definitions stand out. They are:

—— the social production and transmission of identities, meanings, knowledge, beliefs, values, aspirations, memories, purposes, attitudes and understanding;

—— the 'way of life' of a particular set of humans: customs, faiths and conventions; codes of manners, dress, cuisine, language, arts, science, technology, religion and rituals; norms and regulations of behaviour, traditions and institutions.

So, culture is both the medium and the message – the inherent values *and* the means and the results of social expression. Culture enfolds every aspect of human intercourse: the family, the education, legal, political and transport systems, the mass media, work practices, welfare programs, leisure pursuits, religion, the built environment …

It may appear that this culture is such an all-embracing concept that it can have little practical use in the 'real' world – at least, in the world of government. Looking at the above, the question is no longer 'what is culture?' but 'what isn't?' As Judy Spokes, Executive Officer of the Cultural Development Network[5] has put it, culture is both 'overarching and underpinning'. It covers both the values upon which a society is based and the embodiments and expressions of these values in the day-to-day world of that society. But, far from being impractical, I am confident that a consistent application of this view of culture offers new pathways to achieving many of the aims expressed in the current governance debates.

This culture is not the decoration added after a society has dealt with its basic needs. Culture *is* the basic need – it is the bedrock of society.

---

[5] For more information about the Cultural Development Network (Vic) see Appendix 4.

It is through cultural action that we:
— make sense of our existence and the environment we inhabit;
— find common expressions of our values and needs;
— meet the challenges presented by our continued stewardship of the planet.

Without culture, we are, quite literally, not human.

Culture has three aspects. It encompasses:
— our values and aspirations;
— the processes and mediums through which we develop, receive and transmit these values and aspirations;
— the tangible and intangible manifestations of these values and aspirations in the real world[6].

It is this concept of culture that I am confident provides the most useful perspective for public policy development, planning and program implementation.

As I have noted above, this definition of culture embraces all of human behaviour. Nevertheless, some aspects of our way of life are more 'cultural' than others. That is, they constitute the primary fields in which the meaning of our lives is expressed, debated and transmitted. Obviously, meaning is inherent in all our activities, but in some it is deliberately purposeful while in others it is less so. In the section, **Restructuring**, I will examine this issue in greater detail, particularly as it effects the implementation of public programs.

CULTURE IN EVERYDAY USEAGE

Culture appears to have two regularly applied, and quite distinct, meanings when used in public discourse: 'values' on the one hand and a slightly expanded notion of 'the arts' on the other.

These two useages of culture, or what I see as the difference between 'culture' and 'Culture', are well illustrated by perusing the daily press.

My reading of *The Age* and *The Australian* on 1/11/00 came up with:
— an article about Hayden's rationale in defence of his position on Indonesia refers to it as 'cultural sleight of hand';
— an article about apparent language difficulties in the international education sector suggests they be viewed in a 'cultural context';
— Paul Kelly states that the shift of media useage from Irian Jaya to West Papua 'symbolises how far the cultural dynamics have shifted';
— an article about the NSW Government's decision to require that speculative apartment buildings be designed by qualified architects states that 'in a dynamic society, we have to accept that there is a culture and a counter-culture at play – one conservative, the other breaking boundaries';

---

[6] In Grogan, D & Mercer, C *The Cultural Planning Handbook: An essential Australian guide* (1995) St Leonards, Allen & Unwin; page 12, these three aspects of culture are described as the 'mind-set', the 'mediums' and the 'artefacts'.

- a monthly update of new scholarly books (anthropology, history, education, political economy, politics, urban studies) is headlined, 'Inside look at culture's world view';
- an article about the German Christian Democrats' proposals for the integration of foreigners is headlined 'Germans clash over culture question'.

In all these cases, 'culture' simply denotes a value system of some kind.

On the day before, *The Age* published an editorial headed 'Culture for all, and all for culture'; its subhead was: 'The arts, in all their many forms, can and do reach beyond the converted'; its opening sentence: 'The arts – or, to use the broader term, culture – have always been with us...' It went on: 'Yet, all culture, anywhere and in any form, needs one vital ingredient to help create and sustain their [that is, Artists'] values: people. Without audiences, readers, gallery-crawlers, and the sense of understanding and replenishment they provide, the circuit of exposition and perception remains incomplete, and the creation itself is put at risk.'

In this case, Culture refers, quite specifically, to the output of Artists; that is, professional makers of Cultural (in this case, 'artistic') products. It includes neither the artistic practices of communities at large nor the activities commonly described as mass or popular culture, let alone any wider view of culture as the system of values informing society as a whole.

VALUES

I take it as self-evident that humans feel it necesary to make sense of their lives and to conduct themselves on the basis of that sense. This process and its results manifest themselves as a value system – a culture. The social dimensions of this activity are what constitutes a society's culture. One of the biggest issues any society has to face is the role of the state in the shaping of the values that inform both government, and more fundamentally, the values of the entire society.

Public planning, at all tiers of government, is the crucible in which the relationship between state and community is refined and from which the most coherent expression of a society's aspirations may emerge – if, that is, the planning processes are themselves imbued with the values of the society those processes serve.

My starting point is the fact that all acts of public intervention (plans, policy, services, whatever) are fundamentally informed by sets of values. Sometimes these values are formally expressed, more often, they are simply assumed. Sometimes it is even denied that they exist at all. (This last position is not one with which I intend to enter into debate. To me, it is self-evident that the 'market' is not a 'natural' phenomenon. It is an artifice constructed by humans, and as such, embodies the values of its creators in exactly the same way as any other construct does.)

The increasing awareness amongst leaders that socially-held values are at the foundation of society is amply demonstrated.

John Howard, at the Melbourne Press Club on 22/11/00, talked of the values that infuse the Federal Government's vision. He talked of the Government creating 'a correlation between the principles, the priorities and the aspirations that Australians carry within themselves day to day, and the policy development framework of their national government'. He went on to state that these values had 'been applied in a practical way to the deliberations of government'. He then said that 'without fixed principles against which to measure all of the options available, it would simply be impossible to govern effectively'.

Paul Keating, at the University of Technology Sydney on 30/11/00, said, 'nothing is more important to a country than the way it thinks of itself. In other words, the commonly shared model of what its national values and priorities are. Everything else, including economic growth, flows from that' (cf Howard: 'national character is an important factor in achieving prosperity').

It is my contention that formal governance mechanisms need to be developed that facilitate the development, expression and application of the values that our society holds as fundamental to its identity.

Two of the questions that this paper will address are:

—— how can the values held by the instigators of public policy more effectively reflect those of the communities they serve? and

—— how can community values find voice, and affect the values of those that make public policy?

It is not my intention to produce a compendium of contemporary social values or to attempt to identify what sub-set of these might define a uniquely Australian character, but it is important to acknowledge how much work has been undertaken throughout the world to develop an expression of human rights that can be used to establish a globally accepted standard. This work has made us all aware that it is possible, and important, to put into words (and ultimately, into law) a framework of values that underpin the sort of world we wish to live in. This is the beginning of the great cultural challenge. Applying this theory in practice is the never ending continuation of that challenge – culture in action.

Since the end of the second world war, numerous international bodies have developed sets of 'universal' rights to which most nations have been prepared to put their names. A lot of the rhetoric of these declarations is in language that is inaccessible, nevertheless they do give us a starting point. Other sources are more poetic and inspirational. For example, in 1776, the writers of the American Declaration of Independence proclaimed: 'we hold these truths to be self-evident, that all men (sic) are created equal, that they are endowed by their Creator with certain unalienable rights, that among these are life, liberty and the pursuit of happiness' (no mention of wealth). This is a moving encapsulation of a vision worth striving for.

In the reading I've undertaken for this paper, a consistent range of values underpinning the various new planning frameworks has emerged. A summary of these is:

—— participation, engagement and democracy;
—— tolerance, compassion and inclusion;
—— freedom, justice and equality;
—— peace, safety and security;
—— health, wellbeing and vitality;
—— creativity, imagination and innovation;
—— love and respect for the environment.

These might make up a set of 'core values'; that is, the basic, 'universal' values a contemporary society might embrace with unanimous agreement.

The most important thing to note at this point is that this set is not prescriptive. Any useful set of social values has to encourage both change (why else include creativity, imagination and innovation?) and respect for difference and diversity (tolerance, compassion and inclusion).

Whatever overall set we embrace, and the developments to that set that occur over time, is our culture (or at least a culture to which we collectively aspire). To name our shared values, to change them, to embrace or discard them and to apply them is culture at work.

CULTURE AND GOVERNMENT

'Cultural policy is often confused with arts policy.'

David Yencken [7]

Yencken, sometime chair of the Australian Heritage Commission and President of the Australian Conservation Foundation, said this in 1982. With few exceptions, it continues to be true[8].

Perhaps the chief reason for this continuing confusion is that it has been the 'arts lobby' that has led the push for the development of public cultural policies. Understandably, this has meant that, while the rhetoric of cultural policy proponents has used the language of cultural theory (for example, 'culture is the way we live and the way we express ourselves'[9]), when practical action is proposed, the main focus has been on the role the arts can play in the fulfilment of a wide range of public functions.

This arts focus of public cultural policies has been exaggerated over the last decade by an emphasis on 'industry'. In response to developments in overall government directions, the arts (or culture, as the arts had become known) realised that it would have to justify itself as a producer of material wealth, as

---

[7] Yencken, D 'The Deep Dung of Cash: Cultural Policy in Australia' *Overland* 88 (1982).
[8] The most notable exception is *Mapping our Culture: A policy for Victoria* (1991) Melbourne, Government of Victoria. Yencken was a key architect of the the Kirner Government's cultural policy released in July 1991. Few of the ideas in this visionary document were transformed into practice before the change of government in October 1992. It has since disappeared, without trace.
[9] *Councils Enhancing Culture: Report on the Regional Distinctiveness Project with NSW Councils* (1997) Sydney, Local Government & Shires Association of NSW: page 6.

a significant employer, as an industry – 'The strength of our culture depends on sustainable and self-reliant cultural industries'[10]. This emphasis on the economic dimension of culture has caused the focus of policy to be on transactions in the market-place (eg attendances at arts events, sales of arts objects) rather than on wider issues of social meaning, values and aspirations.

This approach has turned in on itself to the point that culture (that is, 'Culture', that is, arts and heritage) have come to be seen as merely an instrument in the toolkit of economic development and social policy. Policy makers, viewing the goal of increased material wealth as an end in itself, use Culture as one of the many avenues through which this end can be achieved. The fact that material wealth itself is but a means for achieving a healthy and happy life is overlooked and the fact that culture is the context in which our aspirations are formed and expressed is ignored. But '[c]ulture's role is not exhausted as a servant of ends – though in the narrow sense of the concept this is one of its roles – but it is the social basis of the ends themselves. Development and the economy are part of a people's culture'[11].

These two useages of 'culture' intertwine in most government cultural instruments. For example, the City of Melbourne's *City Plan*[12] states: 'Culture is essentially about a way of life. It is a celebration of what a community is, where it has come from and where it is going – its identity and memory. It is also about how the City and its community do things and what they value'. The 'vision' informing its *Cultural Policy*[13] concludes with: 'The City of Melbourne will stimulate, support and promote contemporary arts and cultural activities that best demonstrate artistic excellence and innovation, that reflect Melbourne's diverse and living culture, and that maximise community involvement'.

The rhetoric, in virtually all government cultural policy statements, is informed by the 'value system' concept of culture. Yet when it comes to the application of policy, again in virtually all cases, the arts take the main focus – culture becomes Culture.

It may be that this definitional shift between theory and practice is seen as a reasonable and practical response to the problems inherent in applying philosophy to real situations. Whether or not this is the case, I believe that the development of 'whole of government' evaluation frameworks provides a much more effective context in which to situate cultural issues than the discrete policy model[14].

This paper will demonstrate that the 'value system' definition of culture offers public planning a perspective that can clarify many of the issues emerging from the current governance debates.

---

[10] Commonwealth of Australia *Creative Nation: Commonwealth cultural policy* (1994) Canberra, Department of Communication and the Arts: page 81.
[11] From a summary of the visionary publication, World Commission on Culture and Development *Our Creative Diversity* (1995) Paris, UNESCO. A precis of the book's main arguments can be found on http://www.unesco.org/culture/development/wccd/summary/html_eng/index_en.htm
[12] City of Melbourne *City Plan: The City of Melbourne's Municipal Strategic Statement 1999* (1999) Melbourne, City of Melbourne; page 41.
[13] City of Melbourne *Revised Cultural Policy* (1998) Melbourne, City of Melbourne (internal document to the Planning, Development and Environment Committee): page 3.
[14] This issue is dealt with in detail in **'The results of culture'**, below.

DEVELOPMENTS IN THE PUBLIC PLANNING ARENA

The last few years have seen the burgeoning of proposals for new ways to approach public planning. The catchcry 'economic development', which has dominated virtually all aspects of public life for nearly two decades, has been revealed to be an insufficient basis upon which to maintain and/or develop a healthy society. Apart from being questioned as an appropriate end in itself (at the very least, there should be others of equal weight), it is being suggested that it is more of an effect than a cause (as exemplified by the statements of Howard and Keating mentioned previously).

Ecologically sustainable development (ESD), triple bottom line (3BL), quality of life, social capital, community wellbeing, community capacity, integrated local area planning, whole of government planning, the genuine progress indicator, good practice, community indicators, social auditing, liveability, civic engagement and active citizenship are all concepts gaining currency in government circles as ways to augment and enhance an exclusively economic view of the world[15].

In the Australian context, the most comprehensive articulations of these issues are 'Local Agenda 21' and the 'National Strategy for Ecologically Sustainable Development'[16]. These two Federal Government supported initiatives introduce 'sustainable development' and a three-dimensional approach (economic, social and environmental) to public planning.

To varying degrees, all the ideas and methodologies mentioned above are informed by two fundamental tenets:

—— **Sustainability**: resources are not limitless – unregulated exploitation causes degradation and depletion. Unless carefully planned and controlled, pursuing immediate material wealth will inevitably result in long-term poverty and ecological disaster[17].

—— **Wellbeing**: research[18] is demonstrating that, although society as a whole is more materially prosperous than ever before, many of its members feel excluded, powerless and unhappy. What is good for the economy is not necessarily good for society.

All of the new frameworks pay at least lip service to the notion of the community development of the values that will inform the policy that emerges from their application. Some, in particular the community indicators movement, are absolutely committed to a methodology based on grass roots articulation. Others, while recognising the need for community ownership of statements of community-held values, are more circumspect about how this might be achieved. Others are simply systems of measurement attempting to bring to account the interests and/or self-perceptions of previously ignored 'stake-holders'.

---

[15] See Appendix 1 for brief descriptions of some of these frameworks.
[16] See below, '**Ecologically sustainable development and the triple bottom line**' and for detailed descriptions, see Appendix 1: '**Ecologically Sustainable Development and Local Agenda 21**'.
[17] See Yencken, D & Wilkinson, D *Resetting the Compass: Australia's journey towards sustainability* (2000) Collingwood, CSIRO Publishing.
[18] See, for example, Eckersley, R *Quality of Life in Australia : An analysis of public perceptions* (1999) Lyneham, The Australia Institute.

What all have in common is the conviction that there is more to life than corporate profit and that ways must be found to articulate and measure the other-than-financial aspects of human aspiration – to express community values in ways that affect public planning. Furthermore, all, at least implicitly, take a whole-of-government perspective. This approach is perfectly suited to a cultural overlay, despite the fact that none of the current paradigms acknowledge the cultural nature of the issues with which they are dealing.

Nor indeed do any display a rigorous approach to culture at all. Most seem to have tacitly accepted an 'arts plus' assumption about culture. This approach has marginalised the concept of culture and denied theorists and practitioners an extremely effective tool. This limitation, and a way to overcome it, is the major issue that the remainder of this paper will discuss.

Let us now look at the relationship between culture and the key concepts that inform the emerging planning frameworks.

Chapter 2

THE APPLICATION OF CULTURE

I look at how the concept of culture is embedded in, and can enhance, the planning paradigms that are emerging as effective ways of moving towards a society that authentically embodies the values of its citizens.

SUSTAINABLE DEVELOPMENT

'Sustainable development ... is about the achievement on a global scale of three principles: economic development, social justice and ecological responsibilty. These principles exhibit a dialectical tension. Sustainable development is in practice always likely to be a shifting compromise among them. The weight given to each of these principles in different philosophical approaches varies greatly and it may be argued that in some variants only two are present: for instance economic development and ecological responsibilty in market environmentalism, and ecological responsibilty and social jusice in the ecocentric model.'

B. Gleeson and N. Low [19]

In its simplest form, the concept of sustainability embodies a desire that future generations inherit a world at least as bountiful as the one we inhabit. However, how to get there, as is demonstrated above, will always be the subject of constant debate. This debate is about values; it is a cultural debate.

But even more fundamental than arguments about relative priorities is the quite reasonable wish that the value system to which we adhere (or, should I say, aspire) is, in itself, sustainable. Surely it is a legitimate desire to wish that one's culture be enduring, and that it inform the culture of future generations. Not that it exactly replicate itself (a forlorn hope anyway), but that, at least, future generations are aware of the dreams of their forebears.

It is also imperative that this value system embraces sustainability in all its forms. The value system we hear most about in the media is the one that single-mindedly promotes ever increasing consumption. We know this is not sustainable.

What most of us have known all along, and recent studies have affirmed[20], is that there are many values informing our society that run counter to those based simply on the production of goods – that, instead, focus on good. These values need to play a stronger role in the design of public policy.

---

[19] Gleeson, B & Low, N 'Cities as consumers of the world's environment' *Consuming Cities* (2000) London, Routledge; page 6.
[20] See, for example, Eckersley, R *Quality of Life in Australia : An analysis of public perceptions* (1999) Lyneham, The Australia Institute.

Two intertwined issues are at play here:

—— A sustainable society depends upon a sustainable culture. If a society's culture disintegrates, so will everything else. I will argue below that vitality is the single most important characteristic of a sustainable culture.

—— Cultural action is required in order to to lay the groundwork for a sustainable future. I will argue below that the initial strategies that need to be implemented to successfully achieve sustainability must be cultural ones.

> **'Sustainable development and the flourishng of culture are interdependent.'**
>
> ***Principle 1 from the Action Plan formulated at the Intergovernmental Conference on Cultural Policies for Development, Stockholm, 3–4/98*** [21]

WELLBEING

> **'Wellbeing, or welfare, refers to the condition or state of being well, contented and satisfied with life … Wellbeing (and so quality of life) has several components, including physical, mental, social and spiritual. Wellbeing and quality of life are also used in a collective sense to describe how well a society satisfies people's wants and needs.'**
>
> ***Richard Eckersley*** [22]

Wellbeing has become one of the key concepts used to describe the state of a community to which it is legitimate to aspire, or at least towards which public authorities should aim their interventions.

There is considerable overlap between the concepts of wellbeing, life satisfaction, liveability and quality of life. There is also considerable divergence in research and measurement approaches. This divergence can most simply be described as being between a concern with the material conditions that constitute a liveable environment on the one hand and on the subjective sense of life satisfaction among citizens on the other.

For the purposes of this paper, I will concentrate on the latter of these approaches in this section and deal with the former in a following section entitled 'Culture, liveability and quality of life'.

---

[21] This conference, entitled 'The Power of Culture', was a highwater mark in the international debate on cultural policy. See http://www.unesco-sweden.org/Conference/Action_Plan.htm

[22] Eckersley, R (ed) *Measuring Progress:Is life getting better?* (1998) Collingwood, CSIRO Publishing; page 6.

[23] See **'Quality of life, wellbeing, life satisfaction & liveability'** in Appendix 1; also Christie, I & Nash, L (eds) *The Good Life (Demos Collection, Issue 14)* (1998) London, Demos is a collection of essays on the pursuit of happiness that contains comprehensive research references.

While there is no doubt that the satisfaction of material wants and needs makes a significant contribution to community wellbeing, research[23] shows that 'a sense of meaning and purpose is the single attitude most strongly associated with life satisfaction'[24].

A socialised version of this statement would read: a shared sense of meaning and purpose is the single attitude most strongly associated with community wellbeing. The process of arriving at collective meanings is central to the health of a community and indeed is possibly the most important role of government. This has been recognised in the current debates through the introduction of concepts such as 'connectedness' and 'belonging'[25].

Clearly, culture, as I have defined it, has the starring role within this paradigm – one may be sick, hungry, poor and rained upon but still have wellbeing if one feels an active part of an organism that is bigger than oneself. This is not said in an attempt to trivialise Maslow's hierarchy of basic needs but to redress the balance. Bread alone is simply not enough.

A society cannot survive unless it is able to develop and maintain, amongst its constituents, a shared expression of, and commitment to, 'a sense of meaning and purpose'. Developing and maintaining this sense is cultural action.

DIVERSITY

'Difference is not just to be tolerated, but valorized, given value by the dominant culture. Difference addresses the powerful, asserting specific needs, claims, and rights. Difference speaks to us with a collective voice, in the voice of specific "social groups". Thus it is beyond liberalism. The individual voices to whom we have been listening speak not only as individuals but also as and for collectivities. Their claim is to be allowed to be different within an inclusive society. They want to be acknowledged and valued as different within a society of citizens – with the right to make claims on the political community and to participate in it. Difference then is not just different interests, not just a reincarnation of the familiar pluralist politics, but a different way of being in the world. This involves the need, and the right, to give expression to difference in the public sphere.'

Leonie Sandercock [26]

---

[24] From Headey & Wearing, *Understanding Happiness*, quoted in Eckersley, R *Quality of Life in Australia: An analysis of public perceptions* (1999) Lyneham, The Australia Institute; page 18.

[25] 'Belonging' is a problematic concept for non-Indigenous Australians that has been inspirationally examined by Peter Read in *Belonging: Australians. Place and Aboriginal Ownership* (2000) Cambridge, Cambridge University Press. See below **'Culture, belonging and a sense of place'** for further discussion.

[26] Sandercock, L *Towards Cosmopolis* (1998) Chichester, John Wiley & Sons; pages 124–125.

There is, within and around the set of values I identified above, enormous space (and need) for cultural diversity. As Gleeson & Low[27] say, 'freely chosen difference' can only emerge out of a set of basic conditions that are embraced by, and available to, all.

Some basic agreements are an essential aspect of living together but so also is the recognition that difference is an elemental aspect of the human condition. And, in nearly all situations, this is an asset to a vital society, not a threat.

Just as biodiversity is an essential component of ecological sustainability, so is cultural diversity essential to social sustainability. Diverse values should not be respected just because we are tolerant folk, but because we must have a pool of diverse perspectives in order to survive, to adapt to changing conditions, to embrace the future.

And it is not simply the discourse between diverse values that will stimulate our communities to discover new visions. The diversity of mediums of expression and of cultural manifestations are both essential parts of life's rich tapestry and invaluable tools with which to engage with the challenges that will inevitably confront us.

It may require emphasing that cultural diversity is a fact of life; the challenge for the state, and for citizens, is to ensure that this diversity is expressed, reflected, acknowledged, indeed 'valorized' in the mainstream of Australian life. For this to occur, significant changes to the power relations within our society will have to occur – cultural democracy involves the exercise of rights, not simply the availability of opportunity. There are many cultures that don't get a fair run in the public arena; addressing this inequity will need strategies and sensitivities that are courageous, inclusive and culturally aware.

As with all cultural matters, the need to foster diversity is not simply a moral imperative.

'Cultural diversity is integral to social cohesion, human development, peaceful coexistence and the prosperity of societies.'

The Santorini Statement, 3rd Annual Ministerial Meeting of the International Network on Cultural Policy, 9/00 [28]

---

[27] Gleeson, B & Low, N *Australian Urban Planning: New challenges, new agendas* (2000) St Leonards, Allen & Unwin; page 220.
[28] See http://www.pch.gc.ca/network-reseau/santorini/English/Statement.htm. This statement includes a ten point list of 'Cultural Diversity Principles' worth consideration by all public planners.

GLOBALISATION AND DISTINCTIVENESS

We are all one, we are all different. Coping with this contradictory truth is a great challenge.

The effects that globalisation is having on local cultures has generated an enormous amount of discussion[29]. In fact, the role of culture as the bedrock of a society is probably better understood in this context than in any other.

The Canadians and the Europeans (in particular the French) have taken the lead in attempting to limit what is perceived to be the cultural imperialism of the USA. Hollywood and McDonalds have become potent symbols of global homogenisation. On the other hand, there are many who argue that the values embedded in the American Dream are, in fact, appropriate for the development of a global culture[30]. There are yet others who, perhaps optimistically, believe that reaction to (and adaption of) Americanisation is the most powerful force in the regeneration of local cultures.

What is clear is that culture is not a closed system – on one hand we embrace influences from myriad sources, many of which are 'global'; on the other, our response to those influences cannot help but be mediated through our own particular, and unique, experience.

Certainly, an awareness of globalisation has contributed to the rash of 'distinctiveness' projects around the country[31].

There are two aspects to distinctiveness: first is the legitimate recognition that every community has its own specific needs and aspirations and that consequently it is appropriate for government to respond to these in ways specific to the particular circumstances.

The second is a desire to be seen by others as special, even better. This approach, usually driven by a promotion and marketing consciousness, may be useful in the context of attracting industry and tourists to an area, but has little positive value (and may even be a negative contribution) when it comes to communities feeling connected to the manifestations of their own culture.

Perhaps authenticity is a better concept to apply in this context than distinctiveness. That is, it may be more productive to concentrate on ensuring that the cultural manifestations *in* a community have a direct relationship with the culture *of* that community than to obsess on what makes a particular community different from, or better than, any other. We ought to be confident enough by now to know that the inevitable uniqueness of the result will be obvious. The opening ceremony of the 2000 Sydney Olympics is a wonderful example of this approach.

---

[29] See, for example, http://www.globalpolicy.org/globaliz/cultural/index.htm and Schech, S & Haggis, J *Culture & Development: a Critical Introduction* (2000) Oxford, Blackwell Publishers.

[30] Francis Fukuyama is the main proponent of the assertion that liberal democracy and free markets are the best ways to organise human societies.

[31] See, for example, *Councils Enhancing Culture: Report on the Regional Distinctiveness Project with NSW Councils* (1997) Sydney, Local Government & Shires Association of NSW.

ENGAGEMENT, ACTIVE CITIZENSHIP AND CIVIL SOCIETY

'The public life – or civic life – is where we go about working out how we should live together as neighbours, as citizens, as members of the global community – it is where the great dramas of our shared existence are played out.'

Frank Moorhouse [32]

There is an increasing awareness that more and more people are feeling disengaged from 'their' society. It is also recognised that this is not a good situation for the society as a whole nor for those who feel left out. In the context of governance, this issue is paramount.

Involvement is obviously motivated by the belief that one can make a difference, that one's contribution can be effective. In a society so devoted to specialisation that almost all important decisions are delegated to experts, many matters of immediate and crucial concern to citizens are so beyond their influence that even thinking about them guarantees frustration. A sense of powerlessness breeds apathy and resentment. In the contemporary world, with the rhetoric of democracy so pervasive, such feelings have been behind a series of 'people's power' movements all over the globe. It may be a long bow to make comparisons between Solidarity, the Berlin Wall, Marcos and Suharto and conditions in Australia, but there is certainly no doubt that there is a generally perceived lack of connectivity between our political elites and their constituencies.

Communities have a right, as well as a responsibility, to engage with the values that determine the nature of the society of which they are a part. While some communities enjoy considerable influence, the ways for many others are clearly insufficient.

Once again, this is a cultural problem, and one that requires cultural solutions. That is, before it is too late, ways must be found to re-engage the body politic. In a vital society, the meaning we make of our lives is something we do together, not an activity to be left to others, no matter how skilled, or representative, they may claim to be. It is within the power, and a primary responsibility, of government to address this problem. Triennial secret ballots may be an efficient version of democracy but it is increasingly obvious that it has flaws from other perspectives, particularly cultural ones.

It may be that local government is best placed to address this issue. It is the tier of governance closest to the citizenry, and therefore (at least theoretically) the one most in touch with, and capable of being responsive to, its constituency. It is probably the best governance level at which to develop new methodologies of participatory democracy and cultural action. It is ideally placed to stimulate community debate on the values and aspirations that should inform our future, and to plan its actions in direct response to the visions of the community.

---

[32] From an interview in *The Australian's Review of Books*, December 2000.

But this understanding does not absolve other tiers of government from their responsibilities in this area, nor does it insulate them from ballot-box responses to community perceptions of institutional indifference. All levels of government need to enhance their day-to-day connections with their constituencies, to promote an active culture.

> 'The ballot box is not always a good protector of minorities. The ballot box can sometimes be an instrument to legitimise oppression by law... Unlike the majoritarian conception of democracy, Australians of today must appreciate that a modern democracy ensures an effective interaction between the will of the majority and the needs of minorities.'
>
> **Michael Kirby** [33]

CREATIVITY AND INNOVATION

> 'The twentieth century has transformed the entire planet from a finite world of certainties to an infinite world of questioning and doubt. So if ever there was a need to stimulate creative imagination and initiative on the part of individuals, communities and whole societies the time is now. The notion of creativity can no longer be restricted to the arts. It must be applied across the full spectrum of human problem-solving.'
>
> **World Commission on Culture and Development** [34]

We are pattern-makers. That is, we come to understand the world through filtering our perceptions through templates that we learn. This process extends from the basic functions of the brain through to the most rarefied of intellectual discourse. Innovation, creativity, lateral-thinking, insight, intuition and imagination are ways of describing the process of inventing new patterns. This process is crucial to our survival. Brain researchers have tentatively claimed that while the brain's left hemisphere is the site of analysis and logical thought (rationality), it is in the right hemisphere that intuition and its associated functions reside[35]. We are in danger of being a society with half a brain.

The introduction of a cultural context into the public planning framework makes it possible to formally apply a more balanced intellectual process to the business of articulating our visions of the future and devising pathways of achievement.

---

[33] From the *Manning Clark Lecture*, delivered 26/3/01 and quoted in *The Age*, 27/3/01.
[34] From the web summary of WCCD *Our Creative Diversity* (1995) Paris, UNESCO (see earlier for web address).
[35] See the essay, 'Split-brain and the mind' in Gregory, R. L. (ed) *The Oxford Companion to the Mind* (1987) Oxford, Oxford University Press; pages 740–747.

Of course we need rational discourse, but at the same time we must not discount our capacity to arrive at solutions through other means; especially given our awareness of how uncomfortable many communities are with the traditional language of government and bureaucratic discourse.

Creativity and innovation have relatively recently joined the lexicon of public planning buzz words. Their use refers to the discovery of imaginative solutions to pressing problems. In terms of the language of planning, this is a welcome development. In practice, at least in this country, it remains to be seen whether the new language will stimulate new behaviour or simply be used to cloak established methods in fancy trappings. Of note is that innovation has been a cornerstone of arts funding rhetoric for at least two decades without any appreciable shifts in the overall shape of financial distribution.

COMMUNITY BUILDING, COHESION, CAPACITY AND SOCIAL CAPITAL

'Social cohesion involves building shared values and communities of interpretation, reducing disparities in wealth and income, and generally enabling people to have a sense that they are engaged in common enterprise, facing shared challenges and that they are members of the same communities.'

Jane Jenson [36]

These concepts[37] are all built on an awareness that humans are social beings and that we are happiest (and, in general, most productive) when we operate interdependently. All of them refer, in some form or other, to the levels of trust required for people to be able to work together. Some proponents of these ideas depend on a philosophy that claims that community is the ideal site of governance and social initiative – that every level 'above' that is a necessary evil. And that, consequently, the more effective communities are, the less the state will have to intervene. This apparent confluence of anarcho-syndicalism and neo-liberalism in their suspicion of 'big government' has been the subject of much debate, which does not need to be elaborated here.

In the context of this paper, the critical issue is the role of culture in the making of community. Given my definition of culture as the production of social values, it would seem to me to be self-evident that culture is at the foundation of the development of community. Community cohesion is utterly dependent upon the capacity of the individuals within a community to understand, respect and trust one another. These qualities are built through cultural interaction.

Social capital has been called the glue that binds society. A more appropriate phrasing of this metaphor would be:

Cultural capital is the glue that holds a society together; social capital is the lubricant that allows it to operate smoothly.

---

[36] Jenson, J *Mapping Social Cohesion: the State of Canadian Research* (1998) Ottawa. Canadian Policy Research Networks.
[37] See Appendix 1, '**Social capital**' for more information.

The concept of community building has been taken up by a number of State Governments[38]. This may result in some devolution of resources and decision-making, but even so, many other questions remain begged. Particularly issues concerning the potential for socio-economic inequities between communities to be heightened through the promotion of community independence. Clearly, initiative at a community level is to be welcomed and supported, but not if, in the process, the sense of wider social obligations and interdependencies are dissipated.

Which is to say that community building is a two edged sword. A cultural perspective applied to public initiatives in this area will assist in ensuring that while building locally focused networks, a sense of belonging to a wider family is not lost.

LIVEABILITY AND QUALITY OF LIFE

As noted earlier, these ideas focus on the constituents of the environment (natural, constructed and social) that combine to create a place people like and feel attached to. While much of the evaluation in this context has been done with quantitative measures[39] – crime rates, sporting, leisure and shopping facilities, pollution levels, public housing, education levels, health services, public transport and so on, it is becoming clear that other, more intangible, factors affect a community's attachment to their abode.

Concepts such as urban iconography and neighbourhood character are grappling with community perceptions of what is valuable in their surroundings and attempting to allow this awareness to affect the public planning process. Once again, this is culture in action. To recognise it as such will allow these initiatives to be treated in an integrated and co-ordinated manner.

IDENTITY AND CHARACTER

'[C]ultural identity applies to all cultural references through which individuals or groups define or express themselves and by which they wish to be recognised; cultural identity embraces the liberties inherent to human dignity and brings together, in a permanent process, cultural diversity, the particular and the universal, memory and aspiration'

Declaration of Cultural Rights, UNESCO, 1996

Cultural identity does manifest itself in the distinct landscape of a neighbourhood and it is important that the regulation of land use takes the unique physical characteristics (both natural and built) of a precinct into account when determining the parameters of future development. BUT, identity is a far wider, and deeper, concept than simply being a signifier of outward appearance. The concept of identity encompasses *all* the ways we use to remind ourselves, and show others, who we are.

An awareness of the layering and overlaps of identity is crucial to effective

---

[38] See for example, http://www.communitybuilders.nsw.gov.au, a NSW Government site.
[39] See Appendix 1, **'Quality of life, wellbeing, life satisfaction & liveability; objective indicators'**.

planning. There is no doubt that the residents of a city or region identify themselves as being of that place (the big picture) but each has many other identities that gradually focus down until we come to the unique individual. Along the way are large sectors (for example, 'Westies'), suburbs, precincts, streets (for example, Lygon, Smith or Brunswick Street). And that is just identity based upon locale (certainly the easiest to deal with) – we all have a score of other identities: family, gender, work place, age, sporting club, drinking hole, community group, religion, birth place, parents' birth places, educational associations, artistic tastes, fashion choice, sexual preference…

A public plan must facilitate the celebration of all these identities, respect their existence, and use them to stimulate the vitality of the whole. Again there is a dual function in operation here: the promotion of identity is a critical purpose and responsibility in itself, and there are also numerous side benefits. Distinct and confident identities are an integral basis for wellbeing, social cohesion and economic development.

BELONGING AND A SENSE OF PLACE

'I have no right to claim on behalf of non-Aboriginal Australia that all the non-Indigenous are now part of Australia's deep past, nor do I wish to. Belonging ultimately is personal. There are as many routes to belonging as there are non-Aboriginal Australians to find them. My sense of the native-born has come – is coming. It comes through listening but with discernment; through thinking but not asserting; through good times with my Aboriginal friends but not through wanting to be the same as them; through understanding our history but being enriched by the sites of past evil as well as good. It comes from believing that belonging means sharing and that sharing demands equal partnership.'

Peter Read [40]

Read is but one of a panoply of voices that point out that until the issue of Indigenous rights is resolved, the question of how non-Indigenous peoples' sense of connectedness with this country will develop authenticity remains problematic. Which is to say that resolution is an imperative for all of us, not just for Indigenous people.

Belonging is a relatively simple concept to understand in relation to an individual's connection to a group and/or value system. Pride and celebration of place, belonging and connectedness in relation to the physical environment is a little more complex. Especially for those of us who have a sense of connection that spans two hundred years or less. This is not said to call into question place-making as a reasonable planning strategy but simply to remind the reader that no public planning can responsibly avoid taking the issue of Indigenous rights on board.

---

[40] Read, P *Belonging: Australians, Place and Aboriginal Ownership* (2000) Cambridge, Cambridge University Press; page 223.

Beyond stating my conviction that this is the most important issue of our time, there is no more to do in this paper than to emphasise that it is a cultural matter, resolvable only through, in the first instance, cultural action.

ETHICS AND MORALITY

'As the globalization of markets, technology and information sweeps the world, there is a profound need for a new global consensus on basic values. Growing homogenization is countered by accelerating fragmentation: people are brought increasingly together at the same time as they are driven apart. Bridges must be built between them. What principles can provide shared points of reference, the minimal moral guidance the world must heed? Any attempt to formulate global ethics must draw on cultural resources, on people's intelligence, on their emotional experiences, their historical memories and their spiritual orientations.'

World Commission on Culture and Development [41]

There is a resurgence of rhetoric on the need for there to be an overtly ethical dimension to the behaviour of corporations and governments[42]. Morality and ethics are simply a practical and overt application of culture. To view this phenomenon through the lens of culture makes it possible to see how it dovetails with the general thrust of the new paradigms.

PROGRESS AND DEVELOPMENT

'To achieve "ecological growth" we may need to move from an economy of production to an economy of repair – of our damaged society, of our damaged environment, even of our used products. The Swedes call this the "ecocyclic society".'

B. Gleeson & N. Low [43]

Growth, development and progress are concepts that have informed western philosophies of public action for centuries. They had become so ingrained into the fabric that, until relatively recently, the question 'towards what?' was one that was rarely asked. Over the past two decades, if the question had been asked, the answer would have been something like 'more material prosperity'.

The sustainability movement has been at the forefront of the arguments proposing that this goal is not achieveable either on a global scale or in the long term[44]. So what are the goals that more accurately reflect the aspirations

---

[41] From the web summary of WCCD *Our Creative Diversity* (1995) Paris, UNESCO (see earlier for web address).
[42] See, for example, AA1000, the accountability standard developed by the Institute for Social and Ethical Accountability (http://www.AcountAbility.org.uk).
[43] Gleeson, B & Low, N *Australian Urban Planning: New challenges, new agendas* (2000) St Leonards, Allen & Unwin; page 223.
[44] M. Salvaris in his essay 'Citizenship and Progress' (in *Measuring Progress* (1998) Collingwood, CSIRO Publishing; pages 38–43) elequently summarises the debates surrounding thses concepts.

of today's world? As noted earlier, sustainability and wellbeing are the buzz words at the base of the new paradigms.

This means that balance and repair ('ecocylicism' as Gleeson and Low's Swedes put it) are gaining credibility as a way of describing the general direction our world would be wise to be taking.

What has this to do with culture? Apart from the fact that such shifts in view are, in themselves, cultural and that generating community debate around these changes of perception is a cultural act, there remains the way that the concept of culture has been used in conjunction with these terms.

While 'economic development' is beginning to be qualified, 'cultural development' has, so far, not been accorded a similar scrutiny. Apart from the questionable aesthetic dimension to cultural development (which I will deal with below), the main focus of cultural development, as a government instrument, has been economic and 'industrial'. The main thrust has been on expanding the consumption of arts products and of arts production within an industrial model. This has had the effect of transforming culture-making into a market driven commodity consumption activity thereby marginalising (indeed making invisible) its true function. Many government arts agencies may have already become (or at least are in danger of becoming) the cynics of Oscar Wilde's aphorism who know 'the price of everything and the value of nothing'.

As I argue elsewhere, cultural vitality and authenticity may be more useful concepts than cultural development in this new world of sustainability.

VITALITY

A noisy baby is a healthy baby. This child-rearing cliché contains a strong measure of truth when applied to culture. No matter how commendable the values of a society may be, they amount to nothing if the society lacks life, vitality, dynamism and democratic public discourse.

After all, the perceived quality of cultural manifestations is largely a matter of taste. Excellence is an appellation applied to consolidate the taste of a particular group – an attempt to claim absolute ascendancy of particular forms of cultural manifestation in order to consolidate one's own view of the world.

Any reading of history demonstrates how transitory such claims can be. What was considered to be beautiful a decade ago can be embarrassing today. The 'excellence' we choose from the past is often not the same as what was considered excellent at that time, and undoubtedly the same will be true of our era when future generations consider it.

'Development' in this context (that is, in an aesthetic sense) and the striving for excellence that is such a popular rubric amongst public arts agencies are limiting objectives. We need the confidence to facilitate diversity, to believe that, at the end of the day, good will triumph, even though we, at the time, may not recognise it.

We don't need social engineering projects with idealised goals of aesthetic improvement. Instead we need a process of nurture and cultivation. Culture is a fragile and delicate organism. It can easily become atrophied, fragmented, hierarchical, exclusive, lazy, smug, imperialised, passive or one-dimensional.

Continuing health needs constant care – this should be the purpose of public cultural intervention. Not so much a focus on progress, development or excellence as on vitality:

—— culture springs, first and foremost from human interaction – the tangible products of these interactions, no matter how wonderful, are ultimately secondary to the daily exchanges between people;

—— making culture is a daily public event – not just in schools, in the media, in the 'culture houses', but also in the streets, shops, trains and cafes;

—— by our behaviour are we known – this never-ending public process is a society's signature.

Thus a healthy society has a healthy culture and health is meaningless in the absence of life. Culture is not a pile of artefacts – it is us; the living, breathing sum of us.

The manifestations of cultural vitality are the opposites of the list above: robust diversity, tolerant cohesiveness, multi-dimensional egalitarianism, compassionate inclusivity, energetic creativity, open-minded curiosity, confident independence, rude health. Attributes such as these will help us make a future that our children will thank us for.

Governance methodologies will need to have a clear understanding of the role of culture in society if they wish to effectively facilitate the flowering of these qualities in our communities.

THE ARTS

As noted, culture refers not simply to a society's values, but to the **way** these values are developed and expressed. In fact, we cannot know what a society's values are, except by observing their manifestation.

The most difficult challenge for planners may be not so much in identifying a community's values, but in creating the conditions in which that community can autonomously express those values itself. To distribute a questionnaire to householders asking them to tick pre-designed boxes is worse than useless. To liberate the voices, the imaginations and the creativity of the community requires creativity and imagination on the part of the facilitators. Which is why, fundamentally, the arts are such an important aspect of a society's culture.

Before art became an industry manufacturing commodities or an economic development strategy, before it was used as a band-aid to disguise social inequity, before it became a badge of superiority, before it became a decorative embellishment, it was (and remains) the paramount symbolic language through which shifting meanings are presented. This is what has been forgotten in all the attempts to find a place for the arts in government. No attempt to characterise the temper of a time can be meaningful without refering to the arts of that time. After the fact, the arts of an era remain its most accurate reflection.

But this is a view with the advantage of hindsight. What does it have to do with the arts of our own time? Very little really. Our children's children will decide which of our arts reflected our dreams and visions. We cannot know what they will choose.

But what we can learn from history is that a society makes (or discovers) meaning through its arts. In our pursuit of a democracy that really does engage all citizens, that facilitates active participation from the entire spectrum of the body politic, the democratisation of arts practice has to be at the forefront of our strategies.

How can a community develop a conscious, symbolic and effective expression of its own values, meanings and aspirations (that is, culture) without having developed its own creative capacities (that is, arts skills)?

No longer can we be content to leave the creation of meaning to the 'experts'. Yes, it is wonderful to live in a society in which those who choose to devote their entire lives to art are cherished and respected. But this should not diminish our own confidence in making meaning, it should not allow us to become lazy, embarrassed, passive witnesses, silent consumers, mere customers. The new rhetoric is 'engagement' – the first engagement we should have is with arts practice.

Why? Because the arts are the creative imagination at work (and play). Its techniques involve improvisation, intuition, spontaneity, lateral thought, imagination, co-operation, serendipity, trust, inclusion, openness, risk-taking, provocation, surprise, concentration, unorthodoxy, deconstruction, innovation, fortitude and an ability and willingness to delve beneath the surface, beyond the present, above the practical and around the fixed. These are the aspects of human behaviour that social scientists have identified as being the source and manifestation of creativity and innovation – the essential elements for the survival of the species.

An innovative society is open-minded, curious, compassionate and lively; it respects and embraces difference. In so being, it is able to meet every challenge and adapt to changing circumstances. But it can only become so if its citizens are comfortable with applying their creative imaginations to new and changing situations.

A society in which arts practice is not endemic risks its future. The support of professional artists is a laudable policy but far more important is offering all citizens, and their offspring, the opportunity to actively participate in arts practice – to make their own culture.

Creativity, engagement, cohesiveness, wellbeing and respect for difference will be inevitable outcomes.

Communities need access to, and facility with, the tools that come with arts practice in order to find meaningful ways to express their values. Actively involving communities in arts practice (as against product consumption) is the essential starting point to the exercise of generating community-owned expressions of what matters to them. Sitting around making lists is the accountants' way – lists of things that can be measured! How inhibiting is that?

ECOLOGICALLY SUSTAINABLE DEVELOPMENT AND THE TRIPLE BOTTOM LINE

The four pillars of sustainability

'Sustainability, as it has become formally adopted around the world, has not one but three pillars: ecological sustainability, social sustainability and economic sustainability. Some would argue that there should be four pillars and that cultural sustainability should always be included. We agree with this view.'

D. Yencken and D. Wilkinson [45]

Ecologically sustainable development (ESD) with its three dimensions – economic, social and environmental, has become the mantra of contemporary planning[46]. Culture figures hardly at all in this new language. In the rhetoric that surrounds ESD and most of the other new paradigms, one occasionally comes across phrases like 'profound cultural shift' and 'value of cultural diversity'. But really, despite the fact that the meaning of culture exhibited in these phrases meshes exactly with my use of the term, when it comes to practical matters, culture reverts back to its traditional designation of the finer and more refined artefacts of civilisation that one may appreciate after the food is gathered, the roof mended, the road sealed, the workers paid, the children vaccinated, the criminals apprehended and the water purified.

Culture keeps getting guernseys in the pep talks, but when the game starts it always seems to end up on the bench. Perhaps the reasons why this keeps happening aren't all that important, provided that, this time, culture gets a run.

To recapitulate: community wellbeing is built on a shared sense of purpose; values inform action; a healthy society depends, first and foremost, on open, lively and influential cultural activity amongst the communities within it; sustainability can only be achieved when it becomes an enthusiastically embraced part of our culture.

Without a foundation that expressly includes culture, the new frameworks are bereft of the means of comprehending, let alone implementing, the changes they promote. Culture has to be a separate and 'distinct' reference point. Which is to say that the four pillars of sustainability are:

- **Cultural** vitality: wellbeing, creativity, diversity and innovation.
- **Social** equity: justice, engagement, cohesion, welfare.
- **Environmental** responsibility: ecological balance.
- **Economic** viability: material prosperity.

---

[45] Yencken, D & Wilkinson, D. *Resetting the Compass: Australia's journey towards sustainability* (2000) Collingwood, CSIRO Publishing; page 9.

[46] See Appendix 1: '**Ecologically Sustainable Development and Local Agenda 21**' for background information.

This framework provides a balance that is missing from the predominantly trifoil constructs of the moment. Most importantly, it creates a formal space for community discourse, for debate about the values that inform our society.

Let's look at how the existence of this new pillar might impact upon the operations of government.

Chapter 3

THE RESULTS OF CULTURE

I have identified the importance of the function of culture in human development. What remains to be done is to propose practical mechanisms through which culture's importance can deliberatively impact on the planning process itself.

The traditional way that this has been approached is through the development of Cultural Policy. This approach is so endemic that that there is now a formal International Network of Cultural Policy[47] comprising Ministers of Culture from across the globe (Australia is not a member). There are scores of research centres and institutes around the world devoted to the topic, and university departments specialising in teaching the subject.

These are wonderful developments, but I am going to suggest an alternative.

- **Restructuring:** the implementation of public initiatives requires public structures that are able to effectively deal with the purposes informing these initiatives. Current structures do not facilitate this.
- **A 'Cultural Framework':** just as social, environmental and economic filters are applied to all policy, so should it be for culture.
- **Cultural indicators:** to develop such a framework, indicators must be developed.
- **Specific policy development:** to question the need for an overarching cultural policy in no way reduces the need for specific policies in, for example, the arts, communications, education, libraries, sport, the constructed environment, etc.
- **Instrumental initiatives:** while wishing to move on from the perception of culture as a servant of economic and social imperatives, it remains critically important to harness the power of culture to socioeconomic ends when such possibilities do not endanger the vitality and authenticity of the society's culture.
- **Cultural action:** human and social development are culture in motion. Beyond all interventions of the state, we must promote the active participation of communities in the making of their lives.

RESTRUCTURING

Culture is a dynamic process. It is constantly shifting. Keeping in touch with these shifts, making it possible for them to enjoy public expression, facilitating ongoing transmission and the constant public cultural debate go beyond theory. We now enter the realm of implementation.

We have examples. Possibly the most useful is the National Strategy for Ecologically Sustainable Development (NSESD)[48]. This ambitious initiative, begun in 1992, has recently been assessed by the Productivity Commission. The submission of the Australian Conservation Foundation (ACF) to the

---

[47] See the website, http://www.pch.gc.ca/network-reseau/eng.htm
[48] See Appendix 1: **'Ecologically Sustainable Development and Local Agenda 21'** for background information.

Commission's Inquiry stated that 'ESD has never been seriously implemented in Australia. Indeed the prerequisites for its effective implementation are absent. These ... include ... information and accounting frameworks, institutions, departmental structures and functions ...' Many other submissions said similar things and the Commission itself concuded that 'to date overall success of government efforts to implement ESD has been mixed and variable'.

I, like the ACF, am convinced that the 'accounting frameworks, institutions, departmental structures and functions' must be in place *before* wide-ranging policy initiatives of this kind are implemented. Otherwise they will have no hope of success (and a fully developed cultural initiative would be exactly of the same order as the NSESD).

For government to remain in touch with, and responsive to, the cultures of the communities it serves, it needs to identify the prime 'culture-making' social entities and to develop a relationship with these that is consciously 'cultural'. That is, to design, implement and evaluate programs and services that impact on these areas from a cultural perspective – a perspective that focuses on the fact that these are the sites in which, every day, our way of life is being celebrated, explored, passed on, threatened, tested, revisited, examined, developed, expanded, diminished, reinterpreted, reinvented, transformed and adapted – the core centres of vitality.

I contend that there are seven areas of social interaction in which culture (that is, the social generation and transmission of meanings and values) is the prime energiser. Ideally, these areas should be organisationally co-ordinated to achieve maximum effect and responsiveness. It is not difficult to imagine a Cultural Affairs Division (or, at another level, Ministry) with responsibilities across the full range of cultural production:

—— Education and training;
—— Communications and public affairs;
—— The constructed environment and public facilities;
—— Arts;
—— History and heritage;
—— Recreation and leisure;
—— Sport.

In the following description of the action centres of such a Division, I have taken a local government perspective, mainly because it is the least obvious.

EDUCATION AND TRAINING

The primary function of education is the transmission of values; particularly at the post-secondary level, vocational training may be the primary rhetoric informing contemporary education policy but nevertheless far more is happening than simply getting ready to work.

Education does not just occur in schools, colleges and universities. While the formal systems are the responsibility of state and federal governments, there remains enormous space for local governance to fill vacuums, stimulate partnerships, negotiate directly with the educational institutions serving its communities, and to lobby the other tiers on relevant issues.

Literacy, in its widest context (that is, not just the capacity to read, but to use the Internet, to write poetry, to have the skills to use any communication medium), is a basic right. Many of these skills are not currently taught in schools and/or many citizens aren't in a position to attend school.

There is enormous potential for local initiatives. Cultural programs in child-care facilities, the opening up of school resources to communities, the advocating of increased interaction between school children and specialist cultural workers (in the arts, media, design, etc), the integration of post-secondary institutions with their surrounding communities (for example, community access initiatives, outreach programs, addressing students' cultural needs, enhancing the cultural impact of the institutions' physical presence upon their surroundings).

COMMUNICATIONS AND PUBLIC AFFAIRS

Communication is as much about listening as it is about speaking. The communications policy of an organ of government must be as much about how it goes about receiving input as it is about promoting its own affairs or regulating the organs of private and public broadcasting.

Communities have the right to the tools of transmission, in all their diversity, as well as the tools of reception. Many of these tools (national newspapers, television and radio networks) are controlled by interests upon which local government would be hard-pressed to have an effect. Nevertheless, monitoring and advocacy are imperatives. Issues might include community access to mass media exposure opportunities, coverage of local issues and the preparedness of the networks to locally broadcast community-initiated materials.

Other areas of focus within this portfolio would be:

— community-based media: its support, the diversity of those using it, and the diversity of types;
— regulation of advertising;
— libraries: internet access, borrowable materials, outreach programs;
— intra-municipality communications; coverage and effectiveness of both Council-initiated and privately run media interventions.

THE CONSTRUCTED ENVIRONMENT AND PUBLIC FACILITIES

Traditionally this is the bailiwick of the Planning Department, of urban designers, facilities managements and asset protectors. In fact, the world we build is the most profound and effective manifestation of our culture. The nature of the places in which we socially interact deeply affects the ways we feel, think and behave.

The design, regulation, maintenance, management and animation of community centres, parks, reserves and gardens, streets and footpaths, sports arenas and ovals, performing arts centres, playgrounds, swimming pools, town halls, plazas, wilderness areas, community farms, libraries, galleries, museums, historic buildings and transport hubs are essentially cultural acts.

And that is just the amenities traditionally under public auspice. Privately operated sites of public congregation (for example, shopping centres, cinemas, cafes and restaurants, pubs and clubs, gyms and bowling alleys) are at least as important as venues of cultural discourse. A consciousness of this needs to be built in to the attitudes that the public agencies responsible for their regulation bring to the negotiating table.

This branch would engage with everything from pride of place to accessible venues to public art to the sensitive design of built structures and places.

ARTS

The role of the arts was discussed in detail earlier in the paper. To summarise, the arts are the paramount symbolic language through which shifting social meanings are presented. In the context of working towards a more inclusive and engaged democracy, it is active community participation and practice in the arts (rather than the consolidation of professional elites, 'audience development', economic development or cultural tourism) that should be the primary focus here.

It is certainly important to encourage the efforts of those who wish to devote their lives to artistic pursuits, particularly in ensuring that practices that are exploring new synergies are supported. The current overwhelming focus on heritage arts may be holding back the full benefit that a society can achieve from its artistic community. The preponderant concentration of state arts support on institutions ('major organisations') that produce work rooted in our European heritage (opera, ballet, orchestras and the theatre) is a worthy effort to maintain the relevance of these forms to contemporary life, but leaves scant resources for artists who are trying to come to grips with what may become the symbolic languages of the future.

Beyond the co-ordination of specifically artistic programs, it is crucially important that other areas of public administration are able to benefit from the unique contribution that arts practice can provide. The cultural planning initiatives since the early nineties have energetically pursued this direction, particularly in areas like public art, urban renewal and so on and there is a considerable body of excellent documentation available[49]. I will deal further with this issue in the section, 'Instrumental Initiatives'.

HISTORY AND HERITAGE

Knowing where we have come from helps us to discover where we want to go. Our social memory and our repositories of insight and understanding are essential elements to our sense of belonging. Without a sense of our past, we are adrift in an endless present.

The role of the museum and the protection of built heritage are the obvious aspects of this area (both would benefit from creative initiatives concerning their current use, for example, outreach programs, active community interaction). But there is much more that can be done. Perhaps most important is the acknowledgement of the extraordinary diversity upon which

---

[49] For example, Guppy, M (ed) *Better Places, Richer Communities: Cultural Planning and Local Development, a practical guide* (1997) Redfern, Australia Council (the Australia Council is perhaps the major source for material on this topic; see their website: http://www.ozco.gov.au. In Britain, Comedia , http://www.comedia.org.uk, has done considerable work in analysing and documenting this area.

our present is founded. Also critical is an awareness of non-physical heritage – oral history projects and community input into the register of what constitute meaningful icons of heritage are key areas.

RECREATION AND LEISURE

What we do in the breaks between the struggle to survive is profoundly important to our wellbeing, our sense of belonging and connectedness, our understanding of ourselves and our relationships – our culture.

SPORT

The rise of organised sport as we know it today was deliberately invented/codified as a value-teaching mechanism (witness such hoary aphorisms as wars being won on the playing fields of Eton). Because we no longer see this as its primary function does not mean that it has stopped happening. The fact that the behaviour of professional sportspeople is so often the subject of media examination is a clear indication that, despite the transformation of sport into commercial spectacle, there continues to be an expectation that its practitioners are role models.

Equitable community access to public facilities, both as participants and as spectators, appears to be an overlooked area. As does the availability of proficient training opportunities for community-based activities.

The development of sport has mirrored that of the arts. It has become viewed as an industry in which highly specialised experts produce a commodity for sale to passive customers. All sorts of public subsidies support this industry, for ostensibly 'economic development' reasons, while active community participation declines.

Clearly, the major engines of cultural production (along with the family and peer groups) are the education system and the media (including the advertising industry), neither of which take much notice of local government (which is not to say, that if it so chose, local government couldn't develop a quite gingery relationship with these monsters). But, notwithstanding local government's separation from these behemoths, there remains the fact that an essential element of cultural production (perhaps *the* essential element) occurs at the local, day-to-day, street, face-to-face level. Identities are fundamentally forged, tested and developed through visceral human interaction – and it is here that local government can be enormously effective.

Local government is not the branch office of some central bureaucracy, not just the place you go to get your card stamped or your plans approved. It represents, at the closest level, the aspirations of its constituency. Local government's constant and direct interaction with the communities it serves is why its key function is community development; that is, the enhancement of the social connections, interactions and support systems that allow us all to become fulfilled and engaged citizens. At the heart of community development is cultural vitality, for it is only through knowing that we belong and that we share values that we can wholeheartedly get on with our lives.

If the design of the public service reflects the function of culture in our society, it will make it far easier for the activities of government to be guided by, and respond to, the culture of our society.

A 'CULTURAL FRAMEWORK'

Once we accept culture to mean the expression and manifestation of what it means to be human, it becomes obvious why a cultural perspective is the essential basis of all public planning. That is, the first step in a planning process has to be an engagement with the values and aspirations of those who will be affected by the plan; unless we are clear about what the *values* are that inform our vision (plan), then it's unworthy of the name and probably unworkable in its realisation – or, at the very least, likely to generate results at odds with its original (often unvoiced) intentions.

The environmental impact analysis of proposals is a familiar operation. Just as there are social, environmental and economic frameworks (or lenses or filters) through which plans are (or should be) evaluated, so should there be for culture. And just as the basic questions being asked by these frameworks are fairly simple, so too would it be with a cultural framework:

—— What has been the quality of community input into the development of the actual and proposed activities under review?

—— To what extent are these activities reflective of the values and ways of life of the communities upon which they (will) impact?

—— Do these activities improve the capacity of communities to act and interact?

Our public planning procedures need a standard method of assessing the cultural impact of all proposals. If it is accepted that cultural vitality is as essential to a sustainable and healthy society as social equity, environmental responsibility and economic viability and that culture resides in all human endeavour, then we need a way to ensure that all public activity is evaluated from a cultural perspective.

So, rather than the creation of a discrete Cultural Policy, the most effective way forward is the development of a Cultural Framework that can be applied to all policy. Ideally, every activity, program, policy and plan of an entity (for example, a local government council) should be evaluated as to its likely and/or achieved impact on each of the four sustainability domains (acknowledging, of course, that there is significant overlap).

Particularly in the cultural and social settings, realistic evaluation would have to include the analysis of research based on anecdotal evidence emanating from citizens directly involved in, or associated with, the activities under scrutiny, as much of the evidence of change would be self-perceived.

Furthermore, to be realistic and useful, a 'whole of society' approach would need to be taken, as an entity's activities cannot be intelligently assesssed without taking into account the entire environment upon which they impact. Also, long-term measurement procedures would need to be developed as the effects of initiatives will themselves be long-term.

These points are raised by way of noting that wide-ranging, professional and ongoing research is needed as a basis for effective evaluation.

But, however it's done, cultural impact evaluation has to be introduced as a mandatory activity throughout the entire public planning process. Without it we will become an endangered species.

CULTURAL INDICATORS

The development of a cultural framework requires a sense of purpose and direction. Its analytical tools cannot be value free. Our society holds certain ideas dear and these need to overtly inform the perspective that is taken. Only if the values are clearly articulated in the first place can they be debated, modified and developed.

I should also emphasise that community involvement, indeed autonomous input, into both the detail of evaluation criteria and the assessment process, ought to be treated as an essential component of the evaluative system.

As noted earlier, culture has three aspects:

— values (content);

— processes and mediums (practice);

— manifestations (results).

Impact analysis would involve the examination of the community building (or 'vitalisation') effects of a particular action or proposed action over these three areas:

CONTENT

— articulations of communities' identity, aspirations and/or history;

— stimulation of community dialogue around quality of life, sustainabilty and respect for diversity issues;

— raising the profile of universal human rights.

PRACTICE

— level of communities' fluency in cultural[50] processes and mediums;

— level of communities' access to cultural processes and mediums;

— level and types of communities' action in cultural processes and mediums.

RESULTS

— manifestations of community-initiated cultural action;

— public access to presented cultural activity;

— profile of cultural activity;

— range and type of public facilities available for cultural activities;

— level and range of use of public facilities for cultural activities.

---

[50] **Cultural**, in this context, refers to phenomena whose most significant function is to do with the development, reception and/or transmission of community values and aspirations; for example, the arts, urban design, heritage, but also public space, sport, recreation, libraries, the media, the internet and the education system (see '**Restructuring**' for a more comprehensive description of the primary cultural production engines).

Social, environmental and economic evaluators would also be applied to specifically cultural policies and programs: for example, social: impact on social cohesion, community self-determination, capacity-building, etc; economic: nature and levels of public investment, etc.

SPECIFIC POLICY DEVELOPMENT

'Often cultural policy is confined to policy for the arts, with an exclusive emphasis on the pursuit of artistic and institutional excellence. A form of policy handicap ensues, inadvertently diverting debate from the support of diversity, choice and citizen participation to tired questions of "high" versus popular art, professional versus amateur status, or whether craft, folk and other popular art forms should be eligible for support.'

World Commission on Culture and Development [51]

Some of the negative side-effects of cultural policy have been acknowledged. However, I do not believe that the full extent of the potential counter-productivity has been recognised.

The reality is that all policy is cultural. Just as all policy is social, environmental and economic. The moment one attempts to create discrete 'Cultural Policy', one becomes enmeshed in the mire of reductionism. It would appear that once embarking on this path, it is inevitable that one ends up back in arts and heritage territory. For example in 1996, the Swedes developed a set of 'national goals for cultural policy:

—— to safeguard freedom of expression and create genuine opportunities for all to use that freedom;
—— to work to create the opportunity for all to participate in cultural life and cultural experiences and to engage in creative activities of their own;
—— to promote cultural diversity, artistic renewal and quality, thereby counteracting the negative effects of commercialism;
—— to make it possible for culture to be a dynamic, challenging and independent force in society;
—— to preserve and use the cultural heritage;
—— to promote education;
—— to promote international cultural exchange and meetings between different cultures within Sweden.'[52]

This is a commendable set of goals. However the primary entity responsible for the implementation of these goals is the National Council for Cultural Affairs whose areas of responsibility are 'theatre, dance, literature, public libraries, periodicals, museums, exhibitions and visual arts'. This despite the fact that the seven goals set out have ramifications that go far beyond the arts.

---

[51] From Chapter 9 of *Our Creative Diversity*. See below for full reference.
[52] From http://www.kur.se, the site of Statens kulturad, the Swedish Government's Cultural Affairs Department.

Similarly, the five cultural policy objectives recommended by the *'Power of Culture'* conference:
— make cultural policy one of the key components of development strategy;
— promote creativity and participation in cultural life;
— reinforce policy and practice to safeguard and enhance the cultural heritage, tangible and intangible, moveable and immovable, and promote cultural industries;
— promote cultural and linguistic diversity in and for the information society;
— make more human and financial resources available for cultural development;[53]

are a spectacularly concise summation of the core issues – issues that impact on all aspects of government, not just the arts.

My concern is that the call for the creation of a discrete Cultural Policy (rather than the development of a Cultural Framework to stand beside the Social, Environmental and Economic Frameworks upon which all policy should be hung) allows for the following, I fear inevitable, consequences:

— **Territorial disputation**: such an instrument, if it were a comprehensive cultural policy, would embrace (or at least address) virtually all aspects of human endeavour. One would end up with departmental disputes all over the place (public transport is a cultural issue! ... maybe so, but it's really a civil engineering responsibility, and so on).
— **Marginalisation**: it creates the potential for 'cultural matters' to be reduced to arts and heritage, possibly even allowing things like tourism, public space, media and education to escape cultural scrutiny.
— **Delay**: the call for the development of a Cultural Policy provides the potential for 'cultural' matters to be withdrawn from current planning developments and put to the side until more urgent matters are dealt with.

Which is not to say that I am arguing against cultural policy – as I have stated, all policy is cultural – merely against Cultural Policy (at least until such time as a Cultural Framework and Indicators have been developed, and the public service structure has been revamped to reflect the major sites of cultural generation).

Nor am I arguing against policy development within and concerning these major sites. Indeed, there is an urgent need for education, communications, constructed environment, arts, history and heritage, recreation and leisure and sports policies that directly address the issues raised in this paper. Appendix 3 *('Arts indicators')* contains a comprehensive set of items that could inform an arts policy that addressed these issues.

In conclusion, it is my observation that it is the arts community, or at least people working in arts funding agencies, that have led the call for the need

---

[53] See Appendix 2, **The action plan from the 'Power of Culture'** or the website http://www.unesco-sweden.org/Conference/Action_Plan.htm for full details.

for cultural planning and policy development. This has led to the general assumption that a cultural plan will focus on 'Cultural' activities and resources, that is, on matters associated primarily with the arts and with heritage. Yes, such planning addresses matters of 'identity' and 'quality of life', but usually from an aesthetic rather than a sociological perspective. And, more often than not, the subtext has been about promoting the function of the professional artist. This, in itself, is a reasonable aim, but it diminishes the critical importance that a cultural overview has to the conceptualisation of the entirety of public planning.

It is my conviction that this concept of cultural planning is altogether too restrictive because it allows 'cultural' issues to be sidelined (yet again) into a narrow and essentially secondary role. I contend that cultural planning should not be seen as the process of producing a specific framework for the management of narrowly Cultural (that is, 'arts-plus') matters but instead as that aspect of the entire planning process that establishes the values upon which all planning is based.

Traditionally, public planning has been an expert-driven, hermetic practice with a focus derived from civil engineering and quantity surveying. Relatively recently, this approach has been enhanced by movements committed to wider perspectives. To my mind, what these share (even though it is never voiced as such) is a commitment to *cultural action*. That is, to the *social* production of values and the application of those values in the conduct of our society.

Along with these initiatives to extend the traditional public planning models, there has developed a considerable international push to integrate the wide concept of culture with the development policies being pursued by national governments and transnational bodies. UNESCO established the World Commission on Culture and Development (WCCD) in the early nineties which concluded its work with the *'Power of Culture'* conference in Stockholm in 1998[54]. Since then the International Network on Cultural Policy (INCP)[55] has continued to follow through on the massive action plan that arose out of the conference[56].

A great deal of the arguments that I have put in this paper are similar to those articulated by the WCCD, most forcefully put in their publication, *'Our Creative Diversity'*[57]. This book, which appears to have little or no currency in planning or cultural circles in Australia, offers a wonderful international perspective on cultural issues and the essential, and critical function of culture in moving towards a sustainable and fulfilled global society.

While I continue to have doubts concerning the focus on cultural policy as the expected solution to this integrative process, there is no doubt that the international debate provides us with fantastic conceptual tools.

---

[54] See http://www.unesco-sweden.org/conference/index.htm for details of the conference. Australia was represented by an eminent academic and a senior public servant. No politicians attended (unlike many other countries).

[55] See http://www.pch.gc.ca/network-reseau/eng.htm for details. This network revolves around an annual informal meeting of Ministers of Culture. There have been three so far (98,99,00). The Australian Arts Minister has not attended as far as can be ascertained. The latest statement from the INCP can be found on http://www.pch.gc.ca/network-reseau/santorini/English/Statement.htm

[56] The full text of The Action Plan can be found in Appendix 2.

[57] World Commission on Culture and Development *Our Creative Diversity* (1995) Paris, UNESCO.

INSTRUMENTAL INITIATIVES

As I have noted earlier, and has been so eloquently articulated by the WCCD, culture is both bedrock and superstructure. While a Cultural Framework will address whole-of-government fundamentals and specific policies emanating from a Ministry of Cultural Affairs would address the particular issues of its departments, we still need to retain our capacity to realise the potential of cultural activity as a tool for the achievement of goals in social, environmental and economic domains.

This, in fact, has been the traditional function of a great deal of public cultural initiatives and should not be discarded in response to the recognition of culture's wider importance to public planning. The section on the arts in *'Restructuring'* notes the exceptional work that has been done in this area and argues for its continuance.

CULTURAL ACTION

A cultural perspective opens up new avenues of strategic planning. If wellbeing and sustainability are accepted (in principle) as fundamental goals, then there is an enormous amount of work to be done in developing community values, attitudes and behaviour, or at least in promoting the understanding that accepting a principle means nothing unless it has practical manifestations in changes to individual and social behaviour. This is a cultural process – values, beliefs and meanings shifting and altering.

To not recognise that culture and cultural change are at the very heart of this struggle to move on from the language, attitudes and ideologies of a solely economic universe is not to take advantage of perhaps the most effective tool at our disposal.

If the fundamental purpose of governance is to work towards a healthy, safe, tolerant and creative society (rather than just a financially prosperous one), then the recognition of this shift in values is a cultural act. *Articulating shared goals is culture at work.*

The implementation of sustainability measures can only be successful if based on significant shifts in social behaviour. These are dependent on enthusiastic community acceptance of values that are in apparent conflict with many of those in current circulation.

This observation holds true for many of the issues that have gathered general in-principle acceptance in recent times: for example, inclusivity, civic engagement, community wellbeing and social cohesion.

Many of these issues deserve specific public initiatives designed to stimulate community debate and to move towards more democratic forms of governance. Much of the work in these areas is still academy focused (even though it is often state funded); it is time to get out of the laboratory and into the streets.

No amount of government regulation will be be effective unless it is administered in a climate of widespread community commitment to these concepts. This climate can be facilitated by concerted cultural action. It is the responsibility of government to be active (indeed, to take the lead) at this level. The attitude and will of government, particularly local government, will determine the outcomes.

CONCLUSION

— Current government useage and understanding of culture in its planning, service delivery and evaluation activities is limited by its focus on artistic matters. While this has been useful in getting the arts on to the agenda, it has obscured culture's wider value as the context in which a society can come to grips with articulating and manifesting the meanings and purposes which should guide public action. A shift in useage from concepts such as 'development' and 'excellence' to 'authenticity' and 'vitality' when utilising culture in public discourse will open new ways of addressing critical issues.

— Current thinking in the schools of 'post-GDP' evaluation has overlooked and/or understated the role of culture. While tangentially acknowledging that these new paradigms are, in themselves, 'cultural shifts', when it comes down to brass tacks, culture tends to become a lifestyle option rather than the necessity that it is.

— In developing a new governance paradigm and view of what a healthy society needs, cultural vitality has to treated as one of the basic requirements, main conceptual tenets and overriding evaluation streams. Shared meaning and purpose is a basic determinant of social existence. Culture is dynamic – no governance overview will work without an active and ongoing awareness of this reality.

— Conscious cultural action is essential for the achievement of wellbeing and sustainabilty. Unless these issues are creatively addressed within communities, 'top-down' efforts, no matter how well-intentioned, will not achieve their aims.

— The engines of cultural production require a singular and co-ordinated setting within government management structures. Recognising those areas of human organisation that have cultural expression at their core has enormous consequences when it comes to designing governance structures that will facilitate these expressions.

— The first step in integrating a cultural perspective into the public planning process is to develop a cultural framework through which all planning can be evaluated.

— Active community participation in arts practice is an essential component of a healthy and sustainable society. The methodologies of arts practice not only open up fantastic vistas of community expressivity but also, in their application, profoundly contribute to the development of community.

APPENDIX 1:
PUBLIC PLANNING FRAMEWORKS

What follows are brief descriptions of some of the developing conceptual frameworks that are being applied to governance.

CITIZENSHIP AND DELIBERATIVE DEMOCRACY

Concerns that citizens are becoming alienated from the political processes of democracy and/or that these processes have become inappropriate to contemporary life have led to a number of studies attempting to understand the factors necessary to successfully undertake civic renewal. Chief among these, in the Australian context, is the National Citizenship Project[58].

Active community participation in the articulation of shared social goals appears to be the key element, along with the building of community confidence that such expressions will, in fact, effect the operations of society.

Government interest in these issues led to the Senate Legal and Constitutional Reference Committee setting up an inquiry (1993) into the feasibility of developing indicators of citizenship and wellbeing. Its final report endorsed the establishment of such a system[59] and led, in 1998 to the establishment, by the Federal Government, of the Australian Citizenship Council[60]. The Council was asked to report to the Minister for Immigration and Multicultural Affairs on:

—— contemporary issues in Australian citizenship policy and law to be addressed as Australia moves into the new millennium; and

—— how to promote increased community awareness of the significance of Australian citizenship for all Australians, including its role as a unifying symbol.

In February 2000 it released its report which recommended that the following seven principles be recognised as defining and reflecting the civic culture:

—— to respect and care for the land we share;

—— to maintain the rule of law and the ideal of equality under the law of all Australians;

—— to strengthen Australia as a liberal democracy based on universal adult suffrage and freedom of opinion;

—— to uphold the ideal of Australia as a tolerant and fair society;

—— to recognise and celebrate Australia as an inclusive multicultural society which values its diversity;

—— to continue to develop Australia as a society devoted to the well being of its people;

—— to value the unique status of the Aboriginal and Torres Strait Islander peoples.[61]

---

[58] See Salvaris, M 'Citizenship and Progress' in *Measuring Progress* (1998) Collingwood, CSIRO Publishing; pages 35–52. For more information about the National Citizenship Project see the website: http://www.sisr.net/ where material on the Citizen Project Centre for Urban and Social Research can be found.
[59] Senate Legal and Constitutional Reference Committee *National wellbeing: a system of National Citizenship indicators and benchmarks* (1996) Canberra, Parliament of the Commonwealth of Australia.
[60] See http://www.immi.gov.au/citizenship/council.htm for information about the Council.
[61] *Australian Citizenship for a New Century: A Report by the Australian Citizenship Council* (2000).

The search for democratic models that maintain and enhance ongoing citizen involvement in the process of governance is, not surprisingly, most energetically pursued in the USA. Organisations like the Civic Practices Network[62] and CIVICUS: World Alliance for Citizen Participation[63] are extremely active.

COMMUNITY CAPACITY BUILDING

This concept appears to arise out of the free market philosophy of small government and individual self-reliance. Nevertheless it may have genuine potential as a vehicle for community empowerment and engagement. I have yet to find a succinct description of the concept, but, as I understand it, it refers to the development of communities into entities that have the capacity to be cohesive, sustaining and self-reliant (thus reducing the need for the state to intervene).

Certainly the desire to re-vitalise community life is admirable. Provided that community empowerment is taking place in a society that holds equity, tolerance and justice dear, then such tendencies can only be for the good.

COMMUNITY INDICATORS

Community indicators are 'measuring systems, designed, developed, and researched *by the community members themselves*'. According to *Redefining Progress*[64] the two main frameworks in which this movement is operating are sustainability and 'healthy communities or quality of life'.

ECOLOGICALLY SUSTAINABLE DEVELOPMENT AND LOCAL AGENDA 21

In late 1992 the Council of Australian Governments promulgated the National Strategy for Ecologically Sustainable Development (NSESD)[65]. This is a voluntary code which proposes a number of strategies for all tiers of government to address sustainable development issues. In February 2000, the Productivity Commission released the results of its inquiry into the implementation of the Strategy[66]. The material that follows is drawn from that report.

The NSESD aims to meet the needs of Australians today, while conserving our ecosystems for the benefit of future generations. There are three core objectives:

—— enhance individual and community wellbeing and welfare by following a path of economic development that safeguards the welfare of future generations;

---

[62] See their website, http://www.cpn.org/cpn/sections/about_cpn/what_is_cpn.html
[63] See their website, http://www.civicus.org/
[64] See Redefining Progress *The Community Indicators Handbook* (1997) Redefining Progress; these indicators alongwith many others can be found on the web. See below, '**Sustainable Development Indicators (SDIs)**'.
[65] Commonwealth of Australia *National Strategy for Ecologically Sustainable Development* (1992) Canberra, AGPS.
[66] *Productivity Commission Inquiry into the Implementation of Ecologically Sustainable Development by Commonwealth departments and agencies* (2000) Canberra, AusInfo; the report can be downloaded from http://www.indcom.gov.au/inquiry/esd/finalreport/index.html

— provide for equity within, and between, generations; and

— protect biological diversity and maintain essential processes and life-support systems.

Embodied in these core objectives are the three dimensions of ESD – economic, environmental and social.

NSESD was originally endorsed by Commonwealth, State and Territory Governments and representatives of Local Government. Until 1997, the Intergovernmental Committee for ESD was resposible for reviewing progress. At that time it was disbanded and currently no organisation is filling this role.

Local Agenda 21 (LA21) arises out of Chapter 28 of Agenda 21 (also known as the Rio Declaration), the manifesto adopted by the June 1992 United Nations Conference on Environment and Development (also known as the Earth Summit) held in Rio de Janeiro[67]. In 1999, Environs Australia: the Local Government Environment Network, prepared a guide to LA21[68]. The following material is taken from that publication.

Paragraph 28.1 of Agenda 21 states that 'because so many of the problems and solutions being addressed by Agenda 21 have their roots in local activities, the participation and cooperation of local authorities will be a determining factor in fulfilling objectives. Local authorities construct, operate and maintain economic, social and environmental infrastructure, oversee planning processes, establish local environmental policies and regulations, and assist in implementing national and sub-national environmental policies. As the level of governance closest to the people, they play a vital role in educating, mobilising and responding to the public to promote sustainable development.'

Since 1992 there has been constant affirmation of the principles expressed in LA21. In particular the Newcastle Declaration emanating from the 1997 Pathways to Sustainability Conference (an international conference focusing on the challenge of sustainability for local government) and the report from the 1999 Mayor's Pacific Environment Summit in Honolulu strongly endorsed the program.

The program is aimed at implementing sustainable development at the local level. It comprises systems and processes that integrate environmental, economic and social development and is founded on a strong partnership between local government and the community. Its main focus is on community participation.

---

[67] United Nations Conference on Environment and Development, 3-14 June 1992, Rio de Janeiro *Agenda 21* (1992), New York, United Nations.

[68] Cotter, B & Hannan, K *Our Community Our Future: A guide to Local Agenda 21* (1999), Canberra, Commonwealth of Australia. Chapter 28 of Agenda 21 was prepared by the International Council for Local Environment Initiative (ICLEI); see their website: http://www.iclei.org/

GENUINE PROGRESS INDICATOR

'In 1995, Redefining Progress created a more accurate measure of progress, called the Genuine Progress Indicator (GPI). It starts with the same accounting framework as the GDP, but then makes some crucial distinctions: it adds in the economic contributions of household and volunteer work, but subtracts factors such as crime, pollution, and family breakdown. We continue to update the GPI on a yearly basis to document a more truthful picture of economic progress[69].'

In Australia the GPI concept has been embraced by The Australia Institute[70]. They have recently published a 1995–2000 analysis that brings the following factors to account:

— personal consumption;
— income distribution;
— weighted personal consumption;
— public consumption expenditure (non-defensive);
— value of household and community work;
— costs of unemployment;
— costs of underemployment;
— costs of overwork;
— private defensive expenditure on health and education;
— services of public capital;
— costs of commuting;
— costs of noise pollution;
— costs of transport accidents;
— costs of industrial accidents;
— costs of irrigation water use;
— costs of urban water pollution;
— costs of air pollution;
— costs of land degradation;
— costs of loss of native forests;
— costs of depletion of non-renewable energy resources;
— costs of climate change;
— costs of ozone depletion;
— costs of crime;
— costs of problem gambling;
— value of advertising;
— net capital growth;
— net foreign lending[71].

---

[69] See http://www.rprogress.org/progsum/nip/gpi/gpi_main.html
[70] See their website: http://www.tai.org.au
[71] See Hamilton, C Measuring Changes in Economic Welfare; the Genuine Progress Indicator for Australia *Measuring Progress: is life getting better?* (1998) Collingwood, CSIRO Publishing.

GOOD PRACTICE

'Good practice is an evolving response aimed at improving our social environment through integrated strategic planning, undertaken in partnership with Government, local communities and the private sector.

'Good practice in community development seeks to highlight the importance of:

— respecting the unique dignity of the human person and customs;
— developing community through consultation and participation, and networking with other communities;
— a critical understanding of the important relationship between social, cultural, physical and economic environments;
— an appreciation that organisational systems are needed to support the growth of communities and have continuous improvement; and,
— a need for organisational systems to be accountable to the community and to have outcomes measured for efficiency and effectiveness.

'Good practice is a tool for developing community rather than an absolute.'[72]

INTEGRATED LOCAL AREA PLANNING (ILAP)

According to Graham Sansom[73], ILAP is based on these major principles:

— appropriately responding to distinctive local circumstances and needs;
— taking a holistic view of local areas: linking related physical, environmental, economic, social and cultural issues;
— developing shared understanding and visions amongst all those concerned with local communities and their environments;
— co-ordinating the related activities of different departments, organisations and spheres of government;
— using available resources more efficiently and effectively; eliminating duplication and gaps;
— extensively involving the community, non-government organisations and the private sector in planning and management;
— Local Government taking a lead role in implementing these principles.

QUALITY OF LIFE, WELLBEING, LIFE SATISFACTION & LIVEABILITY

These four concepts, along with 'health', overlap considerably in the literature.

Quality of life appears to have accumulated most of its conceptual credentials as a sub-set of health care (where it continues to be an important tool – see below) while at the same time it has become a phrase describing both how

---

[72] Hornby, F (Project Convenor) *Working Together to Develop our Communities: Good Practice & Benchmarking in Local Government Community Development & Community Services* (1999) Local Government Community Services Association of Australia; page 9.
[73] See Graham Sansom P/L *A Guide to Integrated Local Area Planning* (1993) Canberra, Australian Local Government Association.

people feel about themselves and the world (cf life satisfaction and wellbeing, with which it is often used interchangeably) and a measurement of the quality of the physical (natural and constructed) and social environment of a particular place (cf liveability).

Even in health circles, quality of life exhibits these multiple interpretations. For example, mental health has been described as the 'embodiment of social, emotional and spiritual wellbeing'[74] while, on the other hand, it is also used as a concept covering the complex analysis of empirical health data[75].

According to Eckersley[76], 'psychological wellbeing is closely related to meaning in life, with positive life meaning being related strongly to religious beliefs, self-transcendent values, membership in groups, dedication to a cause and clear life goals (Zika and Chamberlain 1992) … Seligman (1990) argues that one necessary condition for meaning is the attachment to something larger than self, and the larger that entity, the more meaning people can derive.'

SUBJECTIVE INDICATORS

Eckersley's analysis of the research in this area is profoundly important (for example see his essay in *The Age,* 18/11/00[77] and his discussion paper for The Australia Institute[78]). Wearing and Headey, in Measuring Progress[79] introduce the concept of 'happy life expectancy' and demonstrate that this correlates with clear social and economic indicators.

The World Health Organisation (WHO) defines quality of life as 'an individual's perception of their position in life in the context of the culture and value systems in which they live and in relation to their goals, expectations, standards and concerns'. It is affected by 'the person's physical health, psychological state, personal beliefs, social relationships and their relationship to salient features of their environment'.

WHO has developed two measuring instruments of quality of life (WHOQOL-100 and WHOQOL-BREF). These 'place primary importance on the perception of the individual'.

WHO has identified four 'domains' of measurement: physical, psychological, social relationships and environment. 'Psychological' includes self-esteem, positive and negative feelings, beliefs, spirituality, etc.

---

[74] From VicHealth's *Mental Health Promotion Plan*, 1999; page 4.
[75] Mathers, C & Douglas, B 'Measuring progress in population health and wellbeing' *Measuring Progress* (1998) Collingwood, CSIRO Publishing; pages 125–155.
[76] Eckersley, R *Quality of Life in Australia : An analysis of public perceptions* (1999) Lyneham, The Australia Institute; page 18.
[77] Eckersley, R 'It's the weltanschaung, stupid!' *The Age* (18/11/00).
[78] Eckersley, R *Quality of Life in Australia : An analysis of public perceptions* (1999) Lyneham, The Australia Institute. This booklet, as well as containing useful analysis, also identifies a wide range of the 'public perception' research that has taken place over the last fifteen or so years. See also Pusey, M 'Incomes, Standards of Living and Quality of Life' *Measuring Progress* (1998) Collingwood, CSIRO Publishing; pages 183-197 and Mackay, H *Turning Point: Australians choosing their future* (1999) Sydney, Macmillan.
[79] Wearing, A.J. & Headey,B 'Who Enjoys Life and Why: Measuring subjective wellbeing' *Measuring Progress* (1998) Collingwood, CSIRO Publishing; page 169.

'OBJECTIVE' INDICATORS

Mathers & Douglas[80] provide an overview of quality of life in the contemporary Australian epidemiological context. They examine traditional indicators such as life expectancy and infant mortality along with more recent concepts such as 'health-adjusted life expectancy' and 'the disabilty adjusted life year'.

The 'liveability' version of quality of life developed in the late sixties in the USA as an attempt to create measures that showed why, although the standard of living was improving (measured with economic indicators), it was clear that significant sectors of the population perceived the quality of their lives as diminishing. This led to the development of quantifiable social indicators. A contemporary version of these ('objective' in that they are a set of measurable phenomena; 'subjective' in that they were ranked through field research) are included in Rogerson's work[81]:

— violent crime rates;
— local health care provision;
— levels of non-violent crime;
— cost of living;
— education provision;
— pollution levels;
— employment prospects;
— housing costs;
— wage levels;
— shopping facilities;
— unemployment levels;
— travel to work times;
— scenic quality of area;
— climate;
— sports facilities;
— leisure opportunities.

Possibly the most interesting manifestations of objective indicators can be found amongst the plethora of community indicators being developed around the world. In these we can observe the conditions that various communities see as the necessities upon which they see their lives being based[82].

In Britain, Local Agenda 21 (see above) issues have been formalised through 1999 and 2000 amendments to the Local Government Act. These give councils the 'powers they need to promote the economic, social and environmental wellbeing of their areas'[83]. Community wellbeing is described thus:

---

[80] Mathers, C & Douglas, B 'Measuring progress in population health and wellbeing' *Measuring Progress* (1998) Collingwood, CSIRO Publishing; pages 125–155.
[81] Rogerson, R *Quality of Life in Britain* (1997) Glasgow, Department of Geography, University of Strathclyde; page 18.
[82] See Redefining Progress *The Community Indicators Handbook* (1997) Redefining Progress.
[83] See http://www.local-regions.detr.gov.uk/consult/wellbeing/01.htm

'Quality of life is intimately bound up with the local environment. It is affected by the availability of jobs, goods, educational and leisure opportunities. Individual health and welfare depend on the quality of public services and the condition of the built and natural environment. Community wellbeing means improving the conditions that help make healthy, contented and prosperous local communities.'

SOCIAL AUDITING

According to the New Economics Foundation[84] in London, who pioneered the technique, social auditing (or more fully, social and ethical accounting, auditing and reporting) assesses the social impact of an organisation, relative to its own aims, and those of its stakeholders. Stakeholders are defined as those people who affect or are affected by the activities of the organisation. These may include, for example, customers, employees, communities, suppliers and the environment.

SOCIAL CAPITAL

Eva Cox describes social capital as 'the processes between people which establish networks, norms and social trust and facilitate co-ordination and co-operation for mutual benefit'[85] and 'the factor which allows collective action in the public sphere and for the common good'[86].

P. Bullen and J Onyx[87] measured social capital in five communities in NSW in 1998. In their interview program, they focused on eight elements:

—— participation in local community;

—— proactivity in a social context;

—— feelings of trust and safety;

—— neighbourhood connections;

—— family and friends connection;

—— tolerance of diversity;

—— value of life;

—— work connections.

The most comprehensive coverage of how concepts of social capital are affecting Australian public policy can be found in *Social Capital and public policy in Australia*[88].

The Social Capital Project (of which Eva Cox is Director) is itself a great model of networking in action[89]. Internationally, the World Bank is an energetic proponent of social capital concepts[90].

---

[84] See their website: http://www.neweconomics.org/
[85] See Cox, E *A Truly Civil Society*, 1995, ABC Books.
[86] From Cox, E 'Building Social Capital' in *Health Promotion Matters*, Vol 4, 1997; quoted in Winter, I (ed) *Social capital and public policy in Australia* (2000) Melbourne, Australian Institute of Family Studies.
[87] See Bullen, P & Onyx, J *Measuring Social Capital in Five Communities in New South Wales: a Practitioner's Guide* (1998) Management Alternatives.
[88] Winter, I (ed) *Social capital and public policy in Australia* (2000) Melbourne, Australian Institute of Family Studies.
[89] See its website: http://www.socialcapital.uts.edu.au/
[90] See their website: http://www.worldbank.org/poverty/scapital/index.html

SUSTAINABLE DEVELOPMENT

'Development that meets the needs of the present without compromising the ability of future generations to meet their own needs'[91].

SUSTAINABLE DEVELOPMENT INDICATORS (SDIs)

The International Institute of Sustainable Development (IISD) describes these as measurements that combine social, economic and environmental trends.

The IISD's website[92] contains a compendium of well over a thousand SDI initiatives, compiled in collaboration with Environment Canada, Redefining Progress, the World Bank and the UN Division of Sustainable Development. Searching this database reveals 68 inititiatives that make some reference to culture and 42 that refer to the arts.

The Commission of Sustainable Development[93] (set up by the UN out of the Rio conference in 1992) lists the following areas (from the Earth Summit; Agenda 21) under 'Social':

—— combating poverty;

—— demographic dynamics and sustainability;

—— promoting education, public awareness and training;

—— protecting and promoting human health;

—— promoting sustainable human settlement development.

TRIPLE BOTTOM LINE

The accounting and reporting framework designed by John Elkington to facilitate the development of his concept of 'sustaining capitalism'. A business tool to assist in 'the simultaneous pursuit of economic prosperity, environmental quality and social justice'[94].

WHOLE OF GOVERNMENT

Quite similar to the integrated local area planning ideas. As I understand it, it is a perspective based on horizontal and vertical co-ordination/integration. That is, that governments and government sub-sets, at all levels, should take into account the activities of their colleagues and be aware that focused initiatives in all areas inevitably impact on areas outside the designated responsibilities of the agency in question.

---

[91] From the World Commission on Environment and Development *Our Common Future: The Brundtland Report* (1987) Oxford, Oxford University Press.
[92] See http://iisd1.iisd.ca/measure/displayintro.asp
[93] See http://www.un.org/esa/sustdev/
[94] See Elkington, J *Cannibals with Forks: the Triple Bottom Line of 21st Century Business* (1997) Oxford, Capstone Publishing. See also the website of his organisation: http://www.sustainability.co.uk/sustainability.htm

APPENDIX 2: THE ACTION PLAN FROM 'THE POWER OF CULTURE'

THE INTERGOVERNMENTAL CONFERENCE ON CULTURAL POLICIES FOR DEVELOPMENT, HELD AT STOCKHOLM, 30 MARCH–2 APRIL 1998[95]

PREAMBLE

1. *Reaffirming the fundamental principles of the Final Declaration adopted by the World Conference on Cultural Policies in Mexico on 6 August 1982, entitled the Mexico City Declaration on Cultural Policies, which stresses 'that in its widest sense, culture may now be said to be the whole complex of distinctive spiritual, material, intellectual and emotional features that characterize a society or social group. It includes not only the arts and letters, but also modes of life, the fundamental rights of the human being, value systems, traditions and beliefs';*

2. *Recalling that the World Decade for Cultural Development stressed the importance of acknowledging the cultural dimension of development; asserting and enhancing cultural identities; broadening participation in cultural life; and promoting international cultural co-operation;*

3. *Conscious of the efforts needed to face the challenges of cultural development and preservation of the diversity of cultures, as expressed in 'Our Creative Diversity', the Report of the World Commission on Culture and Development;*

4. *Emphasizing the need to take account of universal values while recognizing cultural diversity, the importance of national measures to harmonize national cultural policies and the need to preserve the pluralism of grassroots cultural initiatives in order to promote mutual understanding as well as respect and consideration between individuals and nations in view of the risk of disagreements and conflicts;*

5. *Recognizing that in a democratic framework civil society will become increasingly important in the field of culture;*

6. *Considering that one of the functions of cultural policies is to ensure sufficient scope for the flourishing of creative capacities;*

7. *Having regard to the ever more rapid processes of socio-economic, technological and cultural change, and the growing disparities at the national and international level, as well as the importance of respecting copyright and intellectual property in view of the risks and challenges arising from the promotion of cultural industries and trade in cultural products;*

8. *Considering that the activities of UNESCO, as well as the development policies of Member States, should take into account the role of cultural factors;*

---

[95] From http://www.unesco-sweden.org/Conference/Action_Plan.htm

9. *Taking note of the Declaration of the Conference of Ministers of Culture of the Non-Aligned Movement held at Medellin, Colombia, from 3 to 5 September 1997 and the Conclusions of the Panafrican Consultation on Cultural Policies for Development held at Lomé, Togo, from 10 to 13 February 1998, the meeting of ALECSO in Tunis in February 1998, the report entitled 'In from the Margins' prepared under the auspices of the Council of Europe, and the 'Pro Cultura' Charter adopted at Thessaloniki (June 1997);*

RECOGNIZES THE FOLLOWING PRINCIPLES:

1. Sustainable development and the flourishing of culture are interdependent.
2. One of the chief aims of human development is the social and cultural fulfilment of the individual.
3. Access to and participation in cultural life being a fundamental right of individuals in all communities, governments have a duty to create conditions for the full exercise of this right in accordance with Article 27 of the Universal Declaration of Human Rights.
4. The essential aims of cultural policy are to establish objectives, create structures and secure adequate resources in order to create an environment conducive to human fulfilment.
5. The dialogue between cultures appears to be one of the fundamental cultural and political challenges for the world today; it is an essential condition of peaceful coexistence.
6. Cultural creativity is the source of human progress; and cultural diversity, being a treasure of humankind, is an essential factor of development.
7. New trends, particularly globalization, link cultures ever more closely and enrich the interaction between them, but they may also be detrimental to our creative diversity and to cultural pluralism; they make mutual respect all the more imperative.
8. Harmony between culture and development, respect for cultural identities, tolerance for cultural differences in a framework of plural democratic values, socio-economic equity and respect for territorial unity and national sovereignty are among the preconditions for a lasting and just peace.
9. Acceptance of cultural diversity helps to highlight and strengthen intercommunity links rooted in values that can be shared by all the different socio-cultural components of national society.
10. Creativity in societies favours creation, which stems above all from an individual commitment. This commitment is essential to building our future heritage. It is important to preserve and promote the conditions for such creation – in particular the freedom of the creative artist – within every community.
11. The defence of local and regional cultures threatened by cultures with a global reach must not transform the cultures thus affected into relics deprived of their own development dynamics.

12. We must therefore empower all people and communities to harness their creativity and to consolidate and forge ways of living together with others, facilitating genuine human development and the transition to a culture of peace and non-violence.

THE CONFERENCE IN CONSEQUENCE AFFIRMS THAT:

1. Cultural policy, as one of the main components of endogenous and sustainable development policy, should be implemented in co-ordination with policy in other social areas, on the basis of an integrated approach. Any policy for development must be profoundly sensitive to culture itself.

2. The dialogue between cultures should constitute a fundamental aim of cultural policies and the institutions which embody them at the national and international level; universal freedom of expression is vital for this interaction and for effective participation in cultural life.

3. Cultural policies for the coming century must be anticipatory, responding to persistent problems as well as to new needs.

4. Effective participation in the information society and the mastery by everyone of information and communications technology constitute a significant dimension of any cultural policy.

5. Cultural policies should promote creativity in all its forms, facilitating access to cultural practices and experiences for all citizens regardless of nationality, race, sex, age, physical or mental disability, enrich the sense of cultural identity and belonging of every individual and community and sustain them in their search for a dignified and safe future.

6. Cultural policies should aim to create a sense of the nation as a multifaceted community within the framework of national unity – a community rooted in values that can be shared by all men and women and give access, space and voice to all its members.

7. Cultural policies should also aim to improve social integration and the quality of life of all members of society without discrimination.

8. Cultural policies must respect gender equality, fully recognizing women's parity of rights and freedom of expression and ensuring their access to decision-making positions.

9. Government should endeavour to achieve closer partnerships with civil society in the design and implementation of cultural policies that are integrated into development strategies.

10. In an increasingly interdependent world, the renewal of cultural policies should be envisioned simultaneously at the local, national, regional and global levels.

11. Countries should work together to build a world of intercultural communication, information and understanding, in which the diversity of cultural values, ethics and behaviours fosters a genuine culture of peace.

12. Cultural policies should place particular emphasis on promoting and strengthening ways and means of providing broader access to culture for all sectors of the population, combating exclusion and marginalization, and fostering all processes that favour cultural democratization.

13. Cultural policies should recognize the essential contribution that is made by creators to improving the quality of life, to promoting identity and to the cultural development of society.
14. Any cultural policy should take into account all the elements that shape cultural life: creation, preservation of the heritage and dissemination. A balance should be struck between these factors in order to implement an effective cultural policy, but promoting access to culture and its dissemination is impossible without maintaining a creative dynamic safeguarded by effective legislative protection.

I. POLICY OBJECTIVES RECOMMENDED TO MEMBER STATES

On the basis of the preceding principles, the Conference recommends that States adopt the following five policy objectives:

1: TO MAKE CULTURAL POLICY ONE OF THE KEY COMPONENTS OF DEVELOPMENT STRATEGY.

1. Design and establish cultural policies or review existing ones in such a way that they become one of the key components of endogenous and sustainable development.
2. Promote to this end the integration of cultural policies into development policies, in particular as regards their interaction with social and economic policies.
3. Contribute to the elaboration by UNESCO of guidelines for the development of an international research and training agenda with regard to culture and development.
4. Adopt and put into practice a broader vision of national cultural policy in accordance with the actual conditions in each country, and endeavour to encourage the participation of civil society, including the media.
5. Ensure the full involvement of creators and their professional organizations in the realization of this new vision.
6. Encourage the development and improvement of procedures conducive to cross-sectoral co-ordination of cultural policies.
7. Co-operate internationally and regionally in engaging in cultural activities to tackle the challenges of urbanization, globalization and ongoing technological changes.
8. Promote activities designed to raise the awareness of the population and decision-making bodies to the importance of taking into account cultural factors in the process of sustainable development.
9. Promote exchange and dialogue between individuals, the community and countries on the basis of shared values.
10. Endeavour to obtain, where necessary in co-operation with UNESCO, the recognition of the cultural dimension in the next International Development Strategy and to stimulate debate in both the Economic and Social Council (ECOSOC) and the General Assembly of the United Nations.

2: PROMOTE CREATIVITY AND PARTICIPATION IN CULTURAL LIFE.

1. Continue to treat the different components of the nation with the same respect and offer them equal opportunities to flourish, placing the emphasis on local initiatives which reflect the diversity of cultural profiles.

2. Ensure through cultural and urban cultural policies the development of a local, creative and participatory cultural life and pluralistic management of diversity.

3. Promote knowledge and understanding of cultural and linguistic diversity by strengthening the cultural content of formal and non-formal education, in particular by encouraging the learning of one or more foreign languages.

4. Promote new links between culture and the education system so as to ensure full recognition of culture and the arts as a fundamental dimension of education for all, develop artistic education and stimulate creativity in education programmes at all levels.

5. Recognize the need to give particular attention to the implementation of existing international human rights instruments such as the Universal Declaration of Human Rights, the International Covenant on Economic, Social and Cultural Rights and the Vienna Declaration on Human Rights and make an inventory of cultural rights by evaluating existing instruments which relate to cultural rights.

6. Further cultural policies, programmes, institutions and projects in order to ensure the full participation on equal terms of all individuals in society.

7. Pay greater attention to the role of culture in social transformation processes.

8. Give recognition to women's achievements in culture and development and ensure their participation in the formulation and implementation of cultural policies at all levels.

9. Review all cultural policies, programmes and institutions in order to ensure in particular respect for the rights of the child, as well as those of vulnerable groups with special educational and cultural needs; take into account the needs and aspirations of the young – whose new cultural practices in particular should be supported – as well as the elderly who are all too often left out of cultural life.

10. Allocate appropriate resources to education, cultural research and information necessary for devising and implementing cultural policies.

3: REINFORCE POLICY AND PRACTICE TO SAFEGUARD AND ENHANCE THE CULTURAL HERITAGE, TANGIBLE AND INTANGIBLE, MOVEABLE AND IMMOVEABLE, AND TO PROMOTE CULTURAL INDUSTRIES.

1. Renew and reinforce national commitments to applying UNESCO's Conventions and Recommendations on the conservation of the moveable and immoveable heritage, on the safeguarding of traditional and popular culture, and on the status of the artist and linked issues.

2. Strengthen efficiency in the cultural sector through training schemes for national specialists and cultural administrators and managers, and provide equal opportunities for women in these fields.

3. Renew the traditional definition of heritage, which today must be understood as all natural and cultural elements, tangible or intangible, which are inherited or newly created. Through these elements social groups recognize their identity and commit themselves to pass it on to future generations in a better and enriched form.

4. Acknowledge the emergence of new categories in the area of cultural heritage, such as the cultural landscape, the industrial heritage and cultural tourism.

5. Strengthen the study, inventory, registration and cataloguing of heritage, including oral traditions, so as to permit the design of adequate and effective instruments for the implementation of traditional as well as scientific conservation policies.

6. Encourage through all possible legal and diplomatic means the return and/or restitution of cultural property to its countries of origin.

7. Include and ensure the protection of buildings, sites, ensembles and landscapes of cultural value in urban and regional development plans, programmes and policies.

8. Directly involve citizens and local communities in heritage conservation programmes and establish a list of best practices for heritage policies.

9. Ensure that tourism is respectful of cultures and of the environment and that the income it generates is also used for equitably preserving heritage resources and for strengthening cultural development.

10. Give priority to the creation of a network at the national, regional and international level involving artists and administrators of projects and cultural amenities in order to improve access to culture in both quantitative and qualitative terms.

11. Assist artists, designers and craftspeople by clarifying, safeguarding and improving the rights of creators and consolidate these rights in relation to the market, both locally and worldwide, by preventing commercial abuses.

12. Promote the idea that cultural goods and services should be fully recognized and treated as being not like other forms of merchandise.

13. Intensify co-operation between government, the business sector and other civil society organizations in the field of culture by providing the latter with appropriate regulatory frameworks.

14. Prevent illicit traffic in cultural property on a worldwide basis and in particular the acquisition of unprovenanced objects by museums and private collectors.

4: PROMOTE CULTURAL AND LINGUISTIC DIVERSITY IN AND FOR THE INFORMATION SOCIETY.

1. Provide communication networks, including radio, television and information technologies which serve the cultural and educational needs of the public; encourage the commitment of radio, television, the press and the other media to cultural development issues, such as the promotion of local, regional and national cultures and languages, exploration and preservation of the national heritage and promotion of the diversity of cultural traditions and indigenous and national cultural identities, while guaranteeing the editorial independence of the public service media.

2. Consider providing public radio and television and promote space for community, linguistic and minority services, particularly at the local level and with a view to promoting non-violence.

3. Adopt or reinforce national efforts that foster media pluralism and freedom of expression.

4. Take measures to promote the education and training of children in the use of new media technologies and to combat violence and intolerance, by contributing in particular to the activities of centres or institutions specializing in exchanges of information on children and violence on the screen.

5. Promote the development and use of new technologies and new communication and information services, stress the importance of access to information highways and services at affordable prices and the equal use of languages, and encourage the use of new technologies in public services.

6. Promote in addition education conducive to the mastery and creative use of new information technologies among the younger generations as users and producers of messages and content, and give priority to education in civic values and the training of teachers in new technologies.

7. Elaborate policies for the preservation and development of archives, museums, libraries and other information generated and/or collected by governmental and non-governmental institutions, when possible by digitalization, and establish mechanisms to facilitate access to that content, including the promotion of these institutions as centres for information, education and lifelong learning.

8. Promote knowledge of the cultural and natural heritage by the virtual means provided by the new technologies.

9. Recognize the significance of the new media technologies for the work of creative people as well as the key role of artistic creation in building the information society.

10. Co-operate in the domain of audiovisual media, particularly as regards training, and the development and distribution of audiovisual productions.

11. Encourage cultural co-operation, particularly through joint projects in the field of cultural industries (production, investment and transfer of rights).

12. Encourage research on the relationship between culture and its dissemination in the media and through new communication services, and support efforts to co-ordinate, and possibly harmonize, methods of measurement and evaluation of cultural programming in the media.

5: MAKE MORE HUMAN AND FINACIAL RESOURCES AVAILABLE FOR CULTURAL DEVELOPMENT.

1. Seek to maintain or increase investment at the national level in cultural development and commit, where appropriate, a certain percentage of the government budget for this purpose, in accordance with overall development objectives, priorities and plans.
2. Invite local authorities to commit more funds to cultural activities and encourage them to strengthen their role in the field of cultural development.
3. Devise and develop fiscal frameworks for cultural activities in order to promote business support for cultural development, and elaborate mechanisms such as public endowments and revenue-earning projects by cultural institutions and the tourism and sports sectors.
4. Examine all appropriate measures to ensure that government policies take into account their effect or likely effect on the process of cultural development of another country.
5. Invite the United Nations' funds and programmes, in particular the UNDP, the specialized financial institutions and the national and regional financing bodies to increase the financial assistance they provide for development projects with a significant cultural component.

RECOMMENDATIONS TO THE DIRECTOR-GENERAL OF UNESCO

1. Take the present Action Plan into account when preparing UNESCO's future programme.
2. Elaborate a comprehensive strategy for practical follow-up to this Conference including the possibility or not of organizing a World Summit on Culture and Development, with a view to submitting the question to the Executive Board.
3. Encourage the establishment of networks for research and information on cultural policies for development, including study of the establishment of an observatory of cultural policies.
4. Bring the present Action Plan to the attention of the Secretary-General of the United Nations and through him to the General Assembly, with a view to submitting a report on the results of the present Conference to the latter at its 53rd session, in accordance with the provisions of General Assembly resolution 52/197.
5. Communicate the present Action Plan to the Heads of all the Specialized Agencies of the United Nations system, to other intergovernmental organizations, both international and regional, with a view to seeking the inclusion of cultural policy objectives in all their development programmes and activities, in consultation with Member States and with

their approval.

6. Pursue the goal of obtaining the integration of a cultural perspective into the next International Development Strategy and invite the Specialized Agencies to evaluate their development practices and policies in this perspective.

7. Propose to the Executive Board a set of projects promoting reflection, exchanges of experience and the development of joint projects designed to promote cultural policies with a view to sustainable human development.

8. Suggest to the Secretary-General of the United Nations that one year of the Decade for the Eradication of Poverty (1997–2006) be devoted to the connections between culture and development and the elimination of poverty.

9. UNESCO should, in the light of the results of the Earth Summit, the Earth Summit+5 and the Habitat II Conference, develop mechanisms in order to emphasize the vital place of the cultural heritage in the environment and as an important factor for sustainable development.

10. Encourage Member States to lodge with UNESCO their cultural strategies, with a view to furthering exchanges of information, ideas and practices.

11. Elaborate policies, design programmes and allocate and raise extra budgetary funds with a view to intensifying multilateral cultural co-operation for the improvement of research in the area of international co-operation in and for cultural policies and development.

12. Explore ways of further developing co-operation between UNESCO and other international organizations.

13. Pursue the publication by UNESCO of a biennial World Culture Report.

14. Promote the creation of an observatory of linguistic policies.

APPENDIX 3: ARTS INDICATORS

Below is a list of indicators based closely on the work of the RMC Research Corporation[96]. It is specifically focused on the arts, and is what one might reasonably expect out of a process of 'community efforts to track progress towards a desired future'.

The main focus of these indicators is on the connectedness of the arts community to the wider community and on the development of opportunities for community members to actively engage in arts practice. It is taken for granted that the desire of communities to creatively express themselves would be a primary motive in the development of such a framework. Support for the professional arts is nevertheless included but it is secondary to active community participation.

The reason this perspective has been adopted arises directly out of the Community Indicator movement – indicators developed in areas such as governance, health, education and access to services have all manifested this desire for direct involvement over and above an expectation that professional experts will determine, and provide, the necessities of life.

In other words, this is a framework based on assumptions about what the citizenry may want, rather than on assumptions about what a public authority may feel that it should provide.

THE ARTS COMMUNITY'S CONNECTIONS TO LARGER COMMUNITY ISSUES AND EXPECTATIONS:

- types of new and ongoing experiences created by the arts community specifically aimed at community development;
- extent to which members of the arts community embrace working with communities as a fundamental role;
- working artists and arts groups that are active contributors to community life;
- types and numbers of arts projects working with specific communities;
- types and numbers of issue-based arts projects.

COMMUNITY PERCEPTIONS OF THE ARTS:

- recognition of the range of arts practices; for example, folk to fine arts, ballet to hip hop, Beethoven to Ruby Hunter, Nolan to grafitti;
- recognition of the role the arts can play in community development.

COMMUNITY EXPECTATIONS OF THE ARTS COMMUNITY:

- level of community expectations that the arts can be a meaningful reflection of the community's values, history and aspirations;
- community perceptions of the arts community's willingness to work with communities addressing community issues;
- community perceptions of the nature and extent of publically accessible arts resources;

---

[96] See their website: www.rmcres.com

- levels of community involvement in the management of arts organisations;
- community opportunities to influence what arts offerings are available.

CONNECTIONS ACROSS GROUPS/BOUNDARIES:

- types of activities offered by the arts community with the intended purpose of linking groups of people;
- number of activities that examine connections among groups or across issues.

DIVERSITY OF OPPORTUNITIES FOR ARTS PARTICIPATION, INCLUDING OPPORTUNITIES FOR CONTINUOUS AND DEEPENING PARTICIPATION:

- opportunities for community members to fully participate in residency and other community-based arts projects;
- range of types of community contribution offered by arts organisations (including volunteers and 'friends');
- proportion of adults surveyed who report significantly meaningful arts experiences over the past year;
- level of significance of, and satisfaction from, participation;
- perceived accessibility of arts institutions;
- number/location of public art sites;
- low cost opportunities to attend performances and/or view exhibitions and demonstrations.

DIVERSITY OF OPPORTUNITIES FOR YOUTH AND LEVEL AND CONTINUITY OF PARTICIPATION BY YOUTH:

- level and representativeness (for example, neighbourhood, race, ethnicity, language, gender) of participation by children in public school arts programs;
- range of arts visits to schools;
- students who are enriched intellectually and emotionally through experiences with the arts;
- types of non-school arts offerings specifically targeted at youth.

THE ARTS COMMUNITY'S RESPONSE TO CULTURAL DIVERSITY:

- participation reported by members of racial/ethnic subgroups in arts activities;
- level and type of Indigenous arts activities;
- range of arts activities specifically designed with and for cultural sub-groups; for example, women, youth, children, aged, of a particular neighbourhood, homeless, unemployed, incarcerated.

VITALITY OF ARTS OFFERINGS:

- number and nature of community-initiated/controlled arts projects;
- extent to which participation results in inspirational experiences that are technically proficient and meaningful;
- depth of connections between arts resources and citizenry;
- value(s) reflecting community connections that the artist is trying to convey;
- diversity of ways to engage with arts activities; for example, creation, presentation, witness, volunteer.

HEALTH OF THE ARTS COMMUNITY:

- dollar amount of local sales of local artists' works;
- number (and proportion in comparison with aggregate) of new works presented by local artists;
- opportunities for artists to be involved in public design;
- opportunities for artists to pass on their skills in community contexts;
- extent to which local artists gain exposure beyond the municipal boundaries;
- extent of interstate and international exchanges of artists and their work;
- level of investment in public art as a component of building development;
- accumulated sponsorship/philanthropic support for the arts;
- extent of partnerships between and among arts institutions/groups and with the communities in which they are based;
- types of partnership activities;
- level of volunteer opportunities;
- attendance at arts events;
- numbers of artists domiciled and/or working in the municipality;
- numbers of artists in financial difficulties.

OPPORTUNITIES FOR VOCATIONAL ARTS TRAINING:

- for example, apprenticeship, residency, and master class opportunities;
- accessibility of short and long term post secondary arts training programs.

DIVERSITY OF INSTITUTIONS INVOLVED IN THE ARTS, INCLUDING NON-TRADITIONAL EXAMPLES:

- venues of different types offering performances and exhibitions;
- range of arts activities presented free in open air public places;
- commercial and industrial projects with public art components.

ARTS COMMUNITY'S ENGAGEMENT WITH CELEBRATION OF HERITAGE:

—— range of oral history projects;
—— development of historical and culturally significant sites.

SUSTAINABILITY OF THE ARTS COMMUNITY:

—— survival rate of established arts groups;
—— extent to which continued activities are independent of external support or established groups.

MUNICIPAL CONTRIBUTION:

—— local government financial support for arts organizations per capita;
—— types of infrastructural support for the arts community available through local government;
—— events and numbers of days booked for arts events in public facilities;
—— level and nature of community input into policy development;
—— level and nature of local government decision-making on arts matters.

APPENDIX 4:
ABOUT THE AUTHOR AND THE NETWORK

THE AUTHOR

Jon Hawkes is an independent advisor specialising in cultural issues. He was the Director of the Australian Centre of the International Theatre Institute for eight years (91-98), Director of the Community Arts Board of the Australia Council (82-87) and founding member of Circus Oz and the Australian Performing Group.

He can be contacted on 613 9489 2668 or at artslink@vicnet.net.au

THE CULTURAL DEVELOPMENT NETWORK

The Victorian-based Cultural Development Network emerged out of the 'Art and Community: New Century, New Connections' national conference held in Melbourne in October 1999. It advocates the adoption of a cultural framework for public policy that integrates community-based arts as essential to strategies to achieve environmental sustainability and social well-being at the local level. Community cultural development facilitated by local government is a key focus of its programs.

Its Executive Officer is Judy Spokes, an experienced community cultural development advocate and policy maker.

The Network is auspiced by the City of Melbourne as an expression of its capital city role and leadership in local government cultural development. The Network is sponsored by VicHealth and the Australia Council, the Commonwealth Government's arts funding and advisory body.

The Network can be contacted on 613 9658 8850 or at judspo@melbourne.vic.gov.au

BIBLIOGRAPHY

Councils Enhancing Culture: Report on the Regional Distinctiveness Project with NSW Councils (1997) Sydney, Local Government & Shires Association of NSW.

Culture - A Sense of Place: Final Report of the MAV's Cultural Development Project in Victoria, 1994-96 (1997) Melbourne, Municipal Association of Victoria.

The Built Imagination: a City of Prospect Urban Design Project, 1991/92 (1992) Adelaide, Prospect City Council.

The Initiative on Defining, Monitoring & Measuring Social Capital Overview & Program Description (Social Capital Initiative Working Papers Nos 1 & 3) (1998) The World Bank.

The Social Reporting Report (part of the Engaging Stakeholders series) United Nations Environment Program & SustainAbility.

Arts Plus: *East End Art Strategy* (1995) Adelaide, Adelaide City Council.

Australian Bureau of Statistics: *Australian Social Trends 2000* (2000) Canberra, Australian Bureau of Statistics.

Badshah, A: *Our Urban Future: New Paradigms for Equity and Sustainability* (1996) London, Zed Press.

Baldwin, S, Godfrey, C & Propper, C (eds): *Quality of Life: perspectives and policies* (1990) London, Routledge.

Baum, N: *Community Services Count* (1995) Sydney, Local Government & Shires Association (NSW).

Bauman, Z: *Postmodernity and its Discontents* (1997) New York, New York University Press.

Beale, A & Van Den Bosch, A (eds): *Ghosts in the Machine: Women & Cultural Policy in Canada & Australia* (1998) Toronto, Garamond.

Beilharz, P: *Postmodern Socialism: Romanticism, City & State* (1994) Melbourne, Melbourne University Press.

Bennett, T: *Culture: a Reformer's Science* (1998) St Leonards, Allen & Unwin.

Bennholdt-Thomsen, V & Mies, M: *The Subsistence Perspective: Beyond the Globalised Economy* (1999) North Melbourne, Spinifex Press.

Bhabha, H K: *The Location of Culture* (1994) London, Routledge.

Bianchini, F: *City Centres, City Cultures: the Role of the Arts in the Revitalisation of Towns & Cities* (1991) Manchester, Centre for Local Economic Strategies.

Bianchini, F & Ghilardi, S: *Culture and Neighbourhoods: a Comparative Report* (1997) Strasbourg, Council of Europe.

Bianchini, F & Landry, C: *Assessing Urban Vitality & Viability* (1995) Bournes Green, Comedia.

Bianchini, F & Parkinson, M (eds): *Cultural Policy & Urban Regeneration: the West European Experience* (1993) Manchester, Manchester University Press.

Binns, V (ed): *Community & the Arts: History, Theory, Practice* (1991) Leichhardt, Pluto Press.

Bird, J et al: *Mapping the Futures: Local Cultures. Global Change* (1993) London, Routledge.

Blowers A & Evans, B (eds): *Town Planning into the 21st Century* (1997) London, Routledge.

Borja, J & Castells, M: *Local & Global: Management of Cities in the Information Age* (1997) London, Earthscan.

Bourdieu, P: *The Field of Cultural Production: Essays on Art and Literature* (1993) Cambridge, Polity Press.

Bourdieu, P & Passeron J C: *Reproduction in Education, Society & Culture* (1990) London, Sage.

Brecknock, R: *Creative Councils Programme Report 1995* (1995) Adelaide, Local Government Association of South Australia.

Brotchie, J & Batty, J: *Cities in Competition: Productive and Sustainable Cities for the 21st Century* (1995) Melbourne, Longman.

Bullen, P & Onyx, J: *Measuring Social Capital in Five Communities in New South Wales: a Practitioner's Guide* (1998) Sydney, Management Alternatives P/L.

Canadian Council on Social Development: *Social Indicators Launchpad & Repository* (2000) Ottawa, http://www.ccsd.ca/index.html.

Cantell, T: *Helsinki and a Vision of Place* (1999) Helsinki, City of Helsinki Urban Facts.

Cantell, T: *In the Public Interest: Making Art that Makes a Difference in the United States (Social Impact of the Arts: Working Paper 9)* Bournes Green, Comedia.

Cantell, T: *The Total Balalaika Show: Shifting Spaces, Shifting Identities (Social Impact of the Arts: Working Paper 5)* Bournes Green, Comedia.

Castells, M: *The Rise of the Network Society* (1996) Oxford, Blackwell.

Christie,I & Nash, L (eds): *The Good Life (Demos Collection, Issue 14)* (1998) London, Demos.

Church, J: *Melbourne Our City Our Culture: Profiling a City's Arts & Cultural Achievements* (1995) Melbourne, Hyland House.

City of Greater Geelong: *Cultural Vision & Strategy: Draft* (1995) Geelong, City of Greater Geelong.

Coghill, K (ed): *Globalisation & Local Democracy* (1997) Melbourne, Montech

Commonwealth of Australia: *Creative Nation: Commonwealth cultural policy* (1994) Canberra, Department of Communications & the Arts.

Considine, M & Painter, M (eds): *Managerialism: the Great Debate* (1997) Melbourne, Melbourne University Press.

Coombes, P & Cook, N (project directors): *Local Government Cultural Development Collaborative Benchmarking: National Demonstration Project* (1997) Sydney, The Australian Local Government Association & the Australia Council.

Cotter,B & Hannan, K: *Our Community Our Future: a guide to Local Agenda 21* (1999) Canberra, Commonwealth of Australia.

Cox, E: *A Truly Civil Society: 1995 Boyer Lectures* (1995) Sydney, ABC Books.

Craik, J (ed): *Cultural Policy Case Studies* (1997) Brisbane, Australian Key Centre for Cultural & Media Studies.

Cranney, P P & Chance, I: *Roads, Rates, Renaissance: Local Government in the Arts in the Nineties* (1993) Adelaide, SA Community Arts Network.

Cunningham, S: *Framing Culture: Culture & Policy in Australia* (1992) St Leonards, Allen & Unwin.

Daly, H: *Beyond Growth: the Economics of Sustainable Development* (1996) Boston, Beacon Press.

Department of Housing & Urban Development (SA): *Portraits of Planning Handbook: Portraits of Planning Conference* (1995) Adelaide, Community Information Service.

Dirlik, A: *Global / Local: Cultural Production & the Transnational Imaginary* (1996) Durham, Duke University Press.

Donovan, A: *Creative Councils: the South Australian Arts & Local Government Consultancy Project* (1993) Adelaide, Local Government Association of South Australia.

Easterling, D, et al: *Promoting Health by Building Community Capacity: Evidence & Implications for Grant Makers* (1998) Denver, The Colorado Trust.

Eckersley, R (ed): *Measuring Progress: Is Life Getting Better?* (1998) Collingwood, CSIRO Publishing.

Eckersley, R: *Quality of Life in Australia: an Analysis of Public Perceptions (Discussion Paper No 23)* (1999) Canberra, The Australia Institute Ltd.

EIT P/L (ed): *The Cultural Planning Conference* (1991) Mornington, Engineering Publications.

Elkington, J: *Cannibals with Forks: the Triple Bottom Line of 21st Century Business* (1997) Oxford, Capstone Publishing.

Engwicht, D: *Finding the Personality of our Place: Towards a Cultural Development Strategy, Report 1; a Report to the Maroochy Shire Council* (1993) Nambour, Maroochy Shire Council.

Engwicht, D: *Street Reclaiming: Creating Livable Streets & Vibrant Communities* (1999) Leichhardt, Pluto Press.

Eryl Morgan Publications P/L: *Creative Futures, Arts & Cultural Development: a Local Government Strategy for Integrated Planning; a Synopsis* (1991) Australia Council Community Development Unit & Commonwealth Office of Local Government.

Etzioni, A: *The Spirit of Community: Rights, Responsibilities & the Communitarian Agenda* (1995) London, Fontana.

European Task Force on Culture and Development: *In From the Margins: a contribution to the debate on culture and development* (1997) Strasbourg, Council of Europe.

Falk, J et al: *Social Equity & the Urban Environment* (1993) Canberra, AGPS.

Ferber, S et al (eds): *Beasts of Suburbia: Reinterpreting Cultures in Australian Suburbs* (1994) Melbourne, Melbourne University Press.

Finch, L & McConville, C (eds): *Images of the Urban: Conference Proceedings* (1998) Maroochydore, Sunshine Coast University College.

Forster, C: *Australian Cities: Continuity & Change* (1995) Melbourne, Oxford University Press.

Freestone, R (ed): *The Twentieth Century Planning Experience: Proceedings of the Eighth International Planning History Sociey Conference and Fourth Australian Planning/Urban History Conference* (1998) Sydney, University of New South Wales.

Frow, J & Morris, M (eds): *Australian Cultural Studies: a Reader* (1993) St Leonards, Allen & Unwin.

Garnham, N: *Concepts of Culture: Public Policy & the Culture Industries* (1987) Cultural Studies 1.

Gibson, K & Watson, S (eds): *Metropolis Now: Planning & the Urban in Contemporary Australia* (1994) Leichhardt, Pluto Press.

Gleeson, B: *Geographies of Disability* (1999) London, Routledge.

Gleeson, B & Hanley, P (eds): *Renewing Australian Planning? New Challenges, New Agendas* (1998) Canberra, Urban Research Program, Australian National University.

Gleeson, B & Low, N: *Australian Urban Planning: New Challenges, New Agendas* (2000) St Leonards, Allen & Unwin.

Gould, H: *The Art of Survival: Investigating Creativity in Humanitarian Aid & Development (Social Impact of the Arts: Working Paper 3)* Bournes Green, Comedia.

Government of Queensland: *Building Local, Going Global, Queensland.Government Cultural Statement* (1995) Brisbane, Government of Queensland.

Government of Victoria: *Mapping our Culture: a Policy for Victoria* (1991) Melbourne, Victorian Ministry for the Arts.

Graham Sansom P/L: *A Guide to Integrated Local Area Planning* (1993) Canberra, Australian Local Government Association.

Graham Sansom P/L: *Ideas for Integrated Local Area Planning* (1993) Canberra, Australian Local Government Association.

Graham Sansom P/L & Praxis Research (ed): *Better Places, Richer Communites: Local Government, Integrated Planning & Cultural Development* (1994) Redfern, Australia Council.

Grayson, L & Young, K: *Quality of Life in Cities: an overview and guide to the literature* (1994) London, The British Library in association with London Research Centre.

Griffin, J: *wellbeing: its meaning, measurement and moral importance* (1986) Oxford, Oxford University Press.

Grogan, D & Mercer, C: *The Cultural Planning Handbook: An Essential Australian Guide* (1995) St Leonards, Allen & Unwin.

Grootaert, C: *What is Social Capital?* The World Bank.

Gunew, S & Razvi, F (eds): *Culture, Difference & the Arts* (1994) St Leonards, Allen & Unwin.

Guppy, M (ed): *Better Places, Richer Communites (Revised Edition): Cultural Planning & Local Development, A Practical Guide* (1997) Redfern, Australia Council.

Guppy, M: *Glenmore Park Cultural Plan* (1993) Sydney, Penrith City Council.

Halsey, A H et al: *Education, Economy, Culture & Society* (1997) New York, Oxford University Press.

Hamnett, S & Freestone, R (eds): *The Australian Metropolis: a Planning History* (2000) St Leonards, Allen & Unwin.

Hart, M: *Guide to Sustainable Community Indicators (2nd ed)* (1999) North Andover, Hart Environmental Data.

Harvey, D: *Justice, Nature & the Geography of Difference* (1996) Oxford, Blackwell

Harvey, D: *Space of Hope.*

Hawkins, G: *From Nimbin to Mardi Gras: Constructing Community Arts* (1993) St Leonards, Allen & Unwin.

Headon, D, Hooton, J & Horne, D (eds): *The Abundant Culture: Meaning & Significance in Everyday Australia* (1995) St Leonards, Allen & Unwin.

Healey, P: *Collaborative Planning: Shaping Places in Fragmented Societies* (1997) Basingstoke, Macmillan.

Health Education Authority: *A Review of Community Based Arts Projects and Inteventions which Impact on Health and Wellbeing* (1999) London.

Hornby, F (Project Convenor): *Working Together to Develop our Communities: Good Practice & Benchmarking in Local Government Community Development & Community Services* (1999) Local Government Community Services Association of Australia.

Hunter, I: *Culture & Government* (1988) London, Macmillan.

Hunter, I, Meredyth, D, Smith, B & Stokes, G: *Accounting for the Humanities: the Language of Culture & the Logic of Government* (1991) Brisbane, Institute for Cultural Policy Studies, Griffth University.

Jamieson, N & Huxley, M (eds): *Restructuring Difference: Social Polarisation & the City (Working Paper 6)* (1996) Melbourne, Australian Housing & Urban Research Institute.

Jenson, J: *Mapping Social Cohesion: the state of Canadian research* (1998) Ottawa, Canadian Policy Research Networks.

Jewson, N & MacGregor, S (eds): *Transforming Cities: Contested Governance and New Spatial Dimensions* (19967) London, Routledge.

Jordan, J: *Revealing the Heart of our Communities: the Queensland Local Government Cultural Development Strategy* (1996) Brisbane, Local Government Association of Queensland Inc.

Jordan, J: *Trial of the Department of Comunications & the Arts' Cultural Mapping Methodology within Cherbourg Aboriginal Council: Report for DOCA* (1996) Brisbane, Department of Comunications & the Arts.

Jordens, A: *Redefining Australians: Immigration, Citizenship and National Identity* (1995) Sydney, Hale & Iremonger.

Kelly, O, Wojdat, E & Khan, N: *The Creative Bits: The Social Impact of the Arts Using Digital Technology* (1997) Bournes Green, Comedia.

Kenny, S: *Developing Communities for the Future: Community Development in Australia* (1994) Melbourne, Nelson.

Khan, N: *The Tent That Covered the World: Multiculturalism & the V&A Textile Project (Social Impact of the Arts: Working Paper 4)* Bournes Green, Comedia.

Kins, A & Peddie, B: *Planning a Complete Community: a Cultural Planning Guide for Local Government* (1996) Perth, Community Arts Network WA Inc.

Kirshenblatt-Gimblett, B: *Destination Culture: Tourism, Museums & Heritage* (1998) Berkeley, University of California Press.

Lamont, M & Fournier, M (eds): *Cultivating Differences* (1992).

Landry, C: *The Creative City: a Toolkit for Urban Innovators* (2000) London, Earthscan in association with Comedia.

Landry, C, & Bianchini, F: *The Creative City* (1995) London, Demos in association with Comedia.

Landry, C, Greene, L, Matarasso, F & Bianchini, F: *The Art of Regeneration: Urban Renewal Through Cultural Activity* (1996) Bournes Green, Comedia.

Lash, S & Urry, J: *Economies of Signs & Space* (1994) London, Sage.

Lawrence, G, Lyons, K & Momtaz, S (eds): *Social Change in Rural Australia* (1996) Rockhampton, Rural Social & Economic Research Centre, Central Queensland University.

Lewis, M: *Sustainable Development Project Bibliography* (1998) American Planning Association.

Lingayah,S, MacGillivray, A & Raynard,P: *Creative Accounting: Beyond the Bottom Line (Social Impact of the Arts: Working Paper 2)* (1996) Bournes Green, Comedia.

Low, N (ed): *Global Ethics & Environment* (1999) London, Routledge.

Low, N: *Planning, Policy & the State* (1991) London, Unwin – Hyman.

Low, N et al (eds): *Consuming Cities: the Urban Environment in the Global Economy after the Rio Declaration* (2000) London, Routledge.

Low, N & Gleeson, B: *Justice, Society & Nature: an Exploration of Political Ecology* (1998) London, Routledge.

Lynch, R & Veal, A: *Australian Leisure* (1996) South Melbourne, Longman.

Macdonnell, J: *Arts Minister? Government Policy & the Arts* (1992) Sydney, Currency Press.

Macdonnell, J: *Review of Regional Arts Development in New South Wales* (1996) Sydney, NSW Ministry for the Arts.

Mackay, H: *Turning Point: Australians choosing their future* (1999) Sydney, Macmillan.

Matarasso, F: *Defining Values: Evaluating Arts Programs (Social Impact of the Arts: Working Paper 1)* (1996) Bournes Green, Comedia.

Matarasso, F: *Northern Lights: The Social Impact of the Feisean (Gaelic Festivals) (Social Impact of the Arts: Working Paper 6)* Bournes Green, Comedia.

Matarasso, F: *Use or Ornament?: The Social Impact of Participation in the Arts* (1997) Bournes Green, Comedia.

Matthews, G: *Global Culture / Individual Identity: Searching for Home in the Global Supermarket* (2000) London, Routledge.

McGuigan, J: *Culture & the Public Sphere* (1996) London, Routledge.

McKay, G: *DIY Culture: Party & Protest in 90s Britain* (1998) London, Allen & Unwin.

Melbourne City Council: *City Plan: Municipal Strategic Statement* (1999) Melbourne, Melbourne City Council.

Melbourne City Council: *Cultural Policy (Revised Edition)* (1998) Melbourne, Melbourne City Council.

Mercer, C (ed): *Urban & Regional Quality of Life Indicators* (1994) Brisbane, Institute for Cultural Policy Studies, Griffith University.

Mercer, C & Taylor, P: *A Cultural Development Strategy: Towards a Cultural Policy for Brisbane* (1991) Brisbane, Brisbane Council.

Miles, M, Hall, T & Borden I (eds): *The City Cultures Reader* (2000) London, Routledge.

Milner, A: *Cultural Materialism* (1993) Melbourne, Melbourne University Press.

Mitchell, D: *Cultural Geography, a Critical Introduction* (2000) Oxford, Blackwell Publishers.

Moriarty, G: *Taliruni's Travellers: An Arts Worker's View of Evaluation (Social Impact of the Arts: Working Paper 7)* Bournes Green, Comedia.

Mules, W & Miller, H (eds): *Mapping Regional Cultures: Discourses in Social Contexts* (1997) Rockhampton, Rural Social & Economic Research Centre, Central Queensland University.

Mulgan, G & Worpole, K: *Saturday Night or Sunday Morning?: From Arts to Industry – New Forms of Cultural Policy* (1986) Bournes Green, Comedia.

Mullhern, F: *Culture / Metaculture* (2000) London, Routledge.

Murphy, C: *Waterworks: an Exploration of Water Through Public Art by Five Regional Communities* (1999) Adelaide, South Australian Country Arts Trust.

Murphy, P & Watson, S: *Surface City: Sydney at the Millennium* (1997) Leichhardt, Pluto Press.

Norton, A, Latham, M. Sturgess, G & Stewart-Weeks, M: *Social Capital: the Individual, Civil Society & the State (Policy Forum 14)* (1997) Sydney, Centre for Independent Studies.

Nussbaum, M & Glover, J (eds): *Women, Culture and Development* (1995) Oxford, Clarendon Press.

Offer, A (ed): *In Pursuit of the Quality of Life* (1996) Oxford, Oxford University Press.

Ohlin, J: *A Change of Culture: Local Governments Planning for Quality of Life, a Report on Integrated Planning with a Focus on Cultural Development* (1992) Hobart, Municipal Association of Tasmania & the Australian Local Government Association.

Onyx, J & Bullen, P : *Measuring Social Capital in Five Communities in New South Wales: an Analysis (CACOM Working Paper No 41)* (1998) Sydney, Centre for Australian Community Organisations & Management, Uniniversity Technology, Sydney.

Palumbo-Liu, D & Gumbrecht, H U (eds): *Streams of Cultural Capital: Transnational Cultural Studies (Mestizo Spaces)* (1998) Stanford University Press.

Pepper, D: *Eco-socialism: from Deep Ecology to Social Justice* (1993) London, Routledge.

Phillip Institute of Technology Project Team: *Local Government's Role in Arts & Cultural Development* (1991) Melbourne, Local Government & Arts Task Force.

Praxis Research: *The Penrith Community Arts & Cultural Development Review* (1993) Sydney, Penrith City Council.

Prime Minister's Urban Design Task Force: *Urban Design in Australia* (1994) Canberra, AGPS.

Redefining Progress, Tyler Norris Associates & Sustainable Seattle: *The Community Indicators Handbook: Measuring Progress Toward Healthy & Sustainable Communities* (1997) Redefining Progress.

Rees, S, Rodley, G & Stilwell, F (eds): *Beyond the Market: Alternatives to Economic Rationalism* (1993) Leichhardt, Pluto Press.

Rentschler, R (ed): *Shaping Culture* (1998) Geelong, Deakin University Press.

Rogerson, R: *Quality of Life in Britain* (1997) Glasgow, Department of Geography, University of Strathclyde.

Rojek, C & Urry, J (eds): *Touring Cultures: Transformation of Travel & Theory* (1997) London, Routledge.

Roseland, M (ed): *Eco-City: Healthy Communities, Healthy Planet* (1997) Gabriola Island, BC, New Society.

Rowe, D (ed): *Imaging Newcastle: Proceedings of the Imaging Newcastle Symposium* (1996) Newcastle, University of Newcastle.

Rowe, D & Lawrence, G (eds): *Tourism, Leisure, Sport: Critical Perspectives* (1998) Sydney, Hodder Education.

Sandercock, L (ed): *Making the Invisible Visible: a Multicultural History of Planning* (1998) Berkeley, University of California Press.

Sandercock, L: *Towards Cosmopolis: Planning for Multicultural Cities* (1998) Chichester, John Wiley.

Schech, S & Haggis, J: *Culture & Development: a Critical Introduction* (2000) Oxford, Blackwell Publishers.

Self, P: *Rolling Back the Market: Economic Dogma & Political Choice* (1999) Basingstoke, Macmillan.

Sen, A & Nussbaum, M (eds): *The Quality of Life* (1993) Oxford, Oxford University Press.

Share, P (ed): *Communication & Culture in Rural Areas* (1995) Wagga Wagga, Centre for Rural Social Research, Charles Sturt University.

Sibley, D: *Geographies of Exclusion: Society & Difference in the West* (1995) London, Routledge.

Skelton, T & Allen, T (eds): *Culture & Global Change* (1999) London, Routledge

Smyth, P & Cass, B (eds): *Contesting the Australian Way: States, Markets & Civil Society* (1998) Cambridge, Cambridge University Press.

Stephenson, G: *Compassionate Town Planning* (1995) Liverpool, Liverpool University Press.

Stevenson, D: *Agendas in Place: Urban & Cultural Planning for Cities & Regions* (1998) Rockhampton, Rural Social & Economic Research Centre, Central Queensland University.

Stevenson, D: *Arts & Organisation: Making Australian Cultural Policy* (2000) St Lucia, University of Queensland Press.

Stewart-Weeks, M & Richardson, C (eds): *Social Capital Stories: How 12 Australian*

Households Lead Their Lives (Policy Monograph 42) (1998) Sydney, Centre for Independent Studies.

Swanson, G & Wise, P: *Going for Broke: Women's Participation in the Arts & Cultural Industries* (1998) Brisbane, Australian Key Centre for Cultural & Media Policy, Griffith University.

Troy, P (ed): *Australian Cities: Issues, Strategies & Policies for Urban Australia in the 1990s* (1995) Melbourne, Cambridge University Press.

Troy, P (ed): *Serving the City* (1999) Leichhardt, Pluto Press.

Troy, P: *The Perils of Urban Consolidation: a Discussion of Australian Housing and Urban Development Policies* (1996) Leichhardt, The Federation Press.

Turner, G (ed): *Nation, Culture, Text: Australian Cultural & Media Studies* (1993) London, Routledge.

Voysey, P & McKinnon, M: *The Great Yarn Event & Other Stories from Regional Australia* (1998) Port Adelaide, Regional Arts Australia.

Waldren, M (ed): *Future Tense* (1999) St Leonards, Allen & Unwin.

Warringa Council: *Cultural Development Program* (1994) Warringa, Warringa Council.

Watson, S & Gibson, K (eds): *Postmodern Cities & Spaces* (1995) Oxford, Blackwell.

Webber, M & Crooks, M (eds): *Putting the People Last: Government, Services & Rights in Victoria* (1996) Melbourne, Hyland House.

Williams, D: *How the Arts Measure Up: Australian Research into the Social Impact of the Arts (Social Impact of the Arts: Working Paper 8)* Bournes Green, Comedia.

Willis, A: *Illusions of Identity: the Art of Nation* (1993) Sydney, Hale & Iremonger.

Wilson, J et al (eds): *The Australian Welfare State* (1996) Melbourne, Macmillan.

Winikoff, T (ed): *Places not Spaces: Placemaking in Australia* (1995) Sydney, Envirobook.

Winter, I (ed): *Social Capital & Public Policy in Australia* (2000) Melbourne, Australian Institute of Family Studies.

Wood, L: *Healthy Communities: a Review of Relevant Projects & Feasibility for Healthway* (1999) Perth, Healthway.

World Bank Group: *Social Capital Database* (1999) . http://www.worldbank.org/poverty/scapital/index.html

World Commission on Culture and Development: *Our Creative Diversity* (1995) Paris, UNESCO.

Worpole, K: *Towns for People: Transforming Urban Life* (1992) Buckingham, Open University Press.

Worpole, K & Greenhalgh, L: *The Richness of Cities: urban policy in a new landscape* (1999) Stroud, Comedia in association with Demos.

Yencken, D, Fien, J & Sykes, H: *Environment, Education & Society in the Asia Pacific: Local Traditions & Global Discourses* (2000) London, Routledge.

Yencken, D & Wilkinson, D: *Resetting the Compass: Australia's Journey Towards Sustainability* (2000) Collingwood, CSIRO Publishing.

Young, G, Clark, I & Sutherland, J: *Mapping Culture: a Guide for Cultural & Economic Development in Communities* (1995) Canberra, The Commonwealth Department of Communications & the Arts.

Zanetti, P & Colman, J: *Creative Village: Rural Town & Environment Design Manual* (1994) Sydney, Arts Council of NSW.

Zukin, S: *The Cultures of Cities* (1995) Cambridge, Blackwell.